T0306003

Numerical Methods in Finance with C++

Driven by concrete computational problems in quantitative finance, this book provides aspiring quant developers with the numerical techniques and programming skills they need.

The authors start from scratch, so the reader does not need any previous experience of C++. Beginning with straightforward option pricing on binomial trees, the book gradually progresses towards more advanced topics, including non-linear solvers, Monte Carlo techniques for path-dependent derivative securities, finite difference methods for partial differential equations, and American option pricing by solving a linear complementarity problem. Further material, including solutions to all exercises and C++ code, is available online.

The book is ideal preparation for work as an entry-level quant programmer, and it gives readers the confidence to progress to more advanced skill sets involving C++ design patterns as applied in finance.

MACIEJ J. CAPIŃSKI is an Associate Professor in the Faculty of Applied Mathematics at AGH University of Science and Technology in Kraków, Poland. His interests include mathematical finance, financial modelling, computer-assisted proofs in dynamical systems and celestial mechanics. He has authored eight research publications and supervised over 30 MSc dissertations, mostly in mathematical finance.

TOMASZ ZASTAWNIAK holds the Chair of Mathematical Finance at the University of York. He has authored about 50 research publications and four books. He has supervised four PhD dissertations and around 80 MSc dissertations in mathematical finance.

Mastering Mathematical Finance

Mastering Mathematical Finance is a series of short books that cover all core topics and the most common electives offered in Master's programmes in mathematical or quantitative finance. The books are closely coordinated and largely self-contained, and can be used efficiently in combination but also individually.

The MMF books start financially from scratch and mathematically assume only undergraduate calculus, linear algebra and elementary probability theory. The necessary mathematics is developed rigorously, with emphasis on a natural development of mathematical ideas and financial intuition, and the readers quickly see real-life financial applications, both for motivation and as the ultimate end for the theory. All books are written for both teaching and self-study, with worked examples, exercises and solutions.

[DMFM]   *Discrete Models of Financial Markets,*
         Marek Capiński, Ekkehard Kopp

[PF]   *Probability for Finance,*
         Ekkehard Kopp, Jan Malczak, Tomasz Zastawniak

[SCF]   *Stochastic Calculus for Finance,*
         Marek Capiński, Ekkehard Kopp, Janusz Traple

[BSM]   *The Black–Scholes Model,*
         Marek Capiński, Ekkehard Kopp

[PTRM]   *Portfolio Theory and Risk Management,*
         Maciej J. Capiński, Ekkehard Kopp

[NMFC]   *Numerical Methods in Finance with C++,*
         Maciej J. Capiński, Tomasz Zastawniak

[SIR]   *Stochastic Interest Rates,*
         Daragh McInerney, Tomasz Zastawniak

[CR]   *Credit Risk,*
         Marek Capiński, Tomasz Zastawniak

[FE]   *Financial Econometrics,*
         Marek Capiński, Jian Zhang

[SCAF]   *Stochastic Control Applied to Finance,*
         Szymon Peszat, Tomasz Zastawniak

Series editors Marek Capiński, *AGH University of Science and Technology, Kraków*; Ekkehard Kopp, *University of Hull*; Tomasz Zastawniak, *University of York*

Numerical Methods in Finance with C++

MACIEJ J. CAPIŃSKI
AGH University of Science and Technology, Kraków, Poland

TOMASZ ZASTAWNIAK
University of York, York, UK

CAMBRIDGE
UNIVERSITY PRESS

University Printing House, Cambridge CB2 8BS, United Kingdom

One Liberty Plaza, 20th Floor, New York, NY 10006, USA

477 Williamstown Road, Port Melbourne, VIC 3207, Australia

314-321, 3rd Floor, Plot 3, Splendor Forum, Jasola District Centre, New Delhi - 110025, India

79 Anson Road, #06-04/06, Singapore 079906

Cambridge University Press is part of the University of Cambridge.

It furthers the University's mission by disseminating knowledge in the pursuit of education, learning and research at the highest international levels of excellence.

www.cambridge.org
Information on this title: www.cambridge.org/9781107003712

First published 2012

A catalogue record for this publication is available from the British Library

Library of Congress Cataloging in Publication data
Capinski, Marek, 1951–
Numerical methods in finance with C++ / Maciej J. Capinski, Tomasz Zastawniak.
p.   cm. – (Mastering mathematical finance)
Includes index.
ISBN 978-1-107-00371-2 (hard back)
1. Finance – Mathematical models.   2. C++ (Computer program language)
I. Zastawniak, Tomasz, 1976– II. Title.
HG106.C363   2012
332.0285´513 – dc23   2012014213

ISBN 978-1-107-00371-2 Hardback
ISBN 978-0-521-17716-0 Paperback

Additional resources for this publication at www.cambridge.org/9781107003712

To Monika and Nina

Contents

Preface

This volume of the 'Mastering Mathematical Finance' series is all about numerical methods combined with C++ programming skills, driven by concrete computational problems in quantitative finance. It begins with straightforward option pricing on binomial trees, and gradually progresses towards more advanced topics, including non-linear solvers, Monte Carlo techniques for path-dependent derivative securities, finite difference methods for partial differential equations, and American option pricing by solving a linear complementarity problem.

Familiarity with C++ is not a prerequisite. The exposition starts from scratch in that respect. Nonetheless, the learning curve is steep, and some, if only limited, experience of computer programming, in any language, might be helpful. In terms of quantitative finance background, working knowledge of the binomial and Black–Scholes models of the market is sufficient. Prior knowledge of numerical methods is not necessary, though it would give some advantage.

This book takes an accelerated route through C++, picking and choosing whatever programming language tools are required to tackle the job in hand. It is not a substitute for a systematic C++ manual. We recommend that the reader should frequently consult such a manual (or Internet resources) for reference about the finer points of the various C++ constructs.

The emphasis is on solving and implementing numerical problems of increasing complexity that arise in finance. Of equal importance is code design that reflects the structure of such problems, facilitates future extensions and encourages collaboration between programmers. This provides motivation to master both the numerical techniques and programming language at the same time.

One of the aims of this course is to prepare the reader for work as an entry-level quant programmer. It can also be used as a springboard to embark on more advanced texts, for example, the brilliant book by Mark Joshi.[1]

The material has been tried and tested at the University of York, as part of an MSc in Mathematical Finance, both campus-based and by online

---

[1] M. Joshi, C++ *Design Patterns and Derivatives Pricing*, Cambridge University Press 2004.

distance learning, and it has also been taught to final-year undergraduates. We are indebted to our students for their feedback and enthusiasm, constructive criticism and creative ideas, which resulted in many improvements both in the code and the text.

The accompanying C++ code is available on the linked website

`www.cambridge.org/9781107003712`

which also contains solutions to all exercises. Errata and some bonus material will be posted on this website in due course.

1

Binomial pricer

In the **binomial model** the prices of assets evolve in discrete time steps $n = 0, 1, 2, \ldots$. There is a **stock** whose price evolves randomly by moving up by a factor $1 + U$ or down by $1 + D$ independently at each time step, starting from the spot price $S(0)$. As a result, the stock price becomes

$$S(n, i) = S(0)(1 + U)^i (1 + D)^{n-i}$$

at step n and node i in the binomial tree

$$
\begin{array}{cccccc}
 & & & & & \cdots \\
 & & & & i = 3 & \nearrow \\
 & & & & & \searrow \\
 & & & i = 2 & \nearrow & \cdots \\
 & & & & \searrow \\
 & & i = 1 & \nearrow & i = 2 & \nearrow \\
 & & & \searrow & & \searrow \\
 i = 0 & \nearrow & & i = 1 & \nearrow & \cdots \\
 & \searrow & & & \searrow \\
 & & i = 0 & \nearrow & i = 1 & \nearrow \\
 & & & \searrow & & \searrow \\
 & & & i = 0 & \nearrow & \cdots \\
 & & & & \searrow \\
 & & & & i = 0 & \nearrow \\
 & & & & & \searrow \\
 & & & & & \cdots \\
 n = 0 & & n = 1 & & n = 2 & n = 3 \quad \cdots
\end{array}
\qquad (1.1)
$$

where $S(0) > 0$, $U > D > -1$ and $n \geq i \geq 0$. There is also a risk-free security, a **money market account**, growing by a factor $1 + R > 0$ during each time step. The model admits no arbitrage whenever $D < R < U$.

Within the binomial model the price $H(n, i)$ at each time step n and node i of a **European option** with expiry date N and payoff $h(S(N))$ can be computed using the **Cox–Ross–Rubinstein (CRR) procedure**, which proceeds by backward induction:

- At the expiry date N

$$H(N, i) = h(S(N, i)) \tag{1.2}$$

  for each node $i = 0, 1, \ldots, N$.
- If $H(n + 1, i)$ is already known at each node $i = 0, 1, \ldots, n + 1$ for some $n = 0, \ldots, N - 1$, then

$$H(n, i) = \frac{qH(n + 1, i + 1) + (1 - q)H(n + 1, i)}{1 + R} \tag{1.3}$$

  for each $i = 0, 1, \ldots, n$.

Here

$$q = \frac{R - D}{U - D}$$

is the **risk-neutral probability**. In particular, for a **call option** the payoff function is

$$h^{\text{call}}(z) = \begin{cases} z - K & \text{if } z > K, \\ 0 & \text{otherwise.} \end{cases} = (z - K)^+$$

and for a **put option** it is

$$h^{\text{put}}(z) = \begin{cases} K - z & \text{if } z < K, \\ 0 & \text{otherwise.} \end{cases} = (K - z)^+$$

for all $z > 0$, where K is the **strike price**. For more details on pricing European options in the binomial model, see [DMFM].

We are going to develop a simple binomial pricer based on these formulae, working through a number of versions of the code, and adding new features at each step.

1.1 Program shell

We start with an almost empty shell that does just one thing: it displays a brief message on the screen and pauses so that the user can read it.

Listing 1.1 Main01.cpp

```
#include <iostream>                               ❶
using namespace std;                              ❷

int main()                                        ❸
{
    //display message                             ❹
    cout << "Hi there" << endl;                   ❺

    //pause program                               ❹
    char x; cin >> x;                             ❻

    return 0;                                      ❼
}
```

Let us examine this code line by line.

❶ `#include <iostream>`
tells the compiler to locate and read the **header file** `iostream.h` and to include its contents in the program. This header file is part of the **standard library** and handles input–output operations. It is needed here because we want to display a message on the screen.

❷ **Namespaces** prevent inadvertent name clashes and help to group related names together. All names in the standard C++ library are wrapped in a single namespace `std`. The line
`using namespace std;`
makes this namespace available throughout the file. Without it we would have to tell the compiler explicitly that `cout`, `endl`, `cin` belong to the namespace by writing them as `std::cout, std::endl, std::cin`. (Try it!)

❸ `int main()`
is the entry point for the C++ program, which starts by executing the first line enclosed within the curly brackets { and }. Every C++ program must contain exactly one such entry point.

❹ The lines starting with `//` are **comments**. When `//` is encountered anywhere in a line of code, everything to the right of `//` in that line is ignored by the C++ compiler.

❺ When the line of code
`cout << "Hi there" << endl;`
is executed, the **output operator** `<<` sends the text enclosed in

quotation marks to the standard output `cout`, which in the majority of operating systems will be a screen window. This is followed by `endl`, with the effect of writing a new line.

❻ Depending on the system used, the window in which the program is executed may be closed automatically when the program terminates, and this may happen too quickly for the user to read the message. The statements

`char x; cin >> x;`

pause the program until the user enters a character from the keyboard. They may be unnecessary on systems that keep the window open after the program terminates. These statements will be omitted in subsequent versions of the program, but can be inserted if pausing is desirable.

This also shows how to enter input from the keyboard. First, `char x;` declares x to be a **variable** (in fact a location in computer memory) to hold a single character. Then `cin >> x;` instructs the program to wait for input from the keyboard (the user needs to type a character and press *Enter*) and to store the input at x. Here >> is the **input operator**. We do not really need x or anything stored in there, but use it merely as a simple technique to pause the program.

❼ `return 0;`

is finally executed. It terminates the program and returns value 0 to tell the operating system that the program has run successfully. Returning a non-zero value would indicate failure.

1.2 Entering data

We are ready to place some useful code inside the shell to read and check the input data. For good measure, we also compute a couple of things, namely the risk-neutral probability and the stock price at a given time step *n* and node *i*.

Listing 1.2   Main02.cpp

```
#include <iostream>
#include <cmath>                                              ❶
using namespace std;

int main()
{
    double S0,U,D,R;                                          ❷
```

```
//entering data
cout << "Enter S0: "; cin >> S0;                        ❸
cout << "Enter U:  "; cin >> U;
cout << "Enter D:  "; cin >> D;
cout << "Enter R:  "; cin >> R;
cout << endl;

//making sure that 0<S0, -1<D<U, -1<R
if (S0<=0.0 || U<=-1.0 || D<=-1.0 || U<=D               ❹
                             || R<=-1.0)
{
    cout << "Illegal data ranges" << endl;
    cout << "Terminating program" << endl;
    return 1;
}

//checking for arbitrage
if (R>=U || R<=D)                                       ❺
{
    cout << "Arbitrage exists" << endl;
    cout << "Terminating program" << endl;
    return 1;
}

cout << "Input data checked" << endl;
cout << "There is no arbitrage" << endl << endl;

//compute risk-neutral probability
cout << "q = " << (R-D)/(U-D) << endl;                  ❻

//compute stock price at node n=3,i=2
int n=3; int i=2;
cout << "n = " << n << endl;
cout << "i = " << i << endl;
cout << "S(n,i) = " << S0*pow(1+U,i)*pow(1+D,n-i)        ❼
                    << endl;

return 0;
}
```

We focus our attention on the new features in this piece of code.

❶ `#include <cmath>`
loads the header file `cmath.h` so we can use various mathematical functions defined in the standard library. We need it in order to have the power function `pow()` later in the code.

② `double S0,U,D,R;`

declares some variables of type `double` to store floating point input data for the spot price $S(0)$, the up and down returns U, D and the risk-free return R.

In C++ the **type** of every variable must be declared before the variable is used. Apart from `double` there are many other variable types. For example, variables of type `int` are used to store integer numbers. In Listing 1.1 we have already seen a variable of type `char` to hold a single character.

③ `cout << "Enter S0: "; cin >> S0;`

displays a message prompting the user to enter the spot price $S(0)$ and handles the input. There are similar lines of code for entering U, D, R.

④ `if (S0<=0.0 || U<=-1.0 || D<=-1.0 || U<=D`
`                                      || R<=-1.0)`

comes next to verify the integrity of input data, ensuring that $0 < S(0)$, $-1 < D < U$ and $-1 < R$. Here `||` is the **logical OR operator**, and `<=` is the **logical inequality operator**, which checks whether or not the inequality $\leq$ holds between two numbers. If the condition inside the round brackets (and) is satisfied, the lines inside the curly brackets { and } after the **if statement** will be executed, displaying a warning message and terminating the program with return value 1, which indicates failure. If the condition inside the round brackets is not satisfied, the program skips the lines inside the curly brackets and moves on to the following line of code.

⑤ `if (R>=U || R<=D)`

similarly checks for the lack of arbitrage, that is, verifies whether or not $D < R < U$. Once these checks are completed successfully, messages to that effect are displayed and the program proceeds to the next line.

⑥ `cout << "q = " << (R-D)/(U-D) << endl;`

computes and displays the risk-neutral probability $q = \frac{R-D}{U-D}$.

⑦ `cout << "S(n,i) = " << S0*pow(1+U,i)*pow(1+D,n-i)`
`                           << endl;`

computes and displays the stock price $S(n,i) = S(0)(1 + U)^i(1 + D)^{n-i}$ at time step n and node i. The variables `n` and `i` are first declared to be of type `int`, initiated with values 3 and 2, respectively, and displayed, just to illustrate how things work.

Exercise 1.1   Tweak the code in `Main02.cpp` so the user can enter n and i from the keyboard.

1.3 Functions

The various parts of the program perform distinct tasks such as inputting and verifying data, computing the risk-neutral probability, or computing the stock price at a given node of the binomial tree. It is good programming practice to arrange such tasks into separate functions, which is what we do next.

Listing 1.3 Main03.cpp

```cpp
#include <iostream>
#include <cmath>
using namespace std;

//computing risk-neutral probability
double RiskNeutProb(double U, double D, double R)          ❶
{
    return (R-D)/(U-D);
}

//computing the stock price at node n,i
double S(double S0, double U, double D, int n, int i)      ❷
{
    return S0*pow(1+U,i)*pow(1+D,n-i);
}

//inputting, displaying and checking model data
int GetInputData(double& S0,                               ❸
                 double& U, double& D, double& R)
{
    //entering data
    cout << "Enter S0: "; cin >> S0;
    cout << "Enter U: "; cin >> U;
    cout << "Enter D: "; cin >> D;
    cout << "Enter R: "; cin >> R;
    cout << endl;

    //making sure that 0<S0, -1<D<U, -1<R
    if (S0<=0.0 || U<=-1.0 || D<=-1.0 || U<=D
                                        || R<=-1.0)
    {
        cout << "Illegal data ranges" << endl;
        cout << "Terminating program" << endl;
        return 1;
    }

    //checking for arbitrage
    if (R>=U || R<=D)
```

```
    {
        cout << "Arbitrage exists" << endl;
        cout << "Terminating program" << endl;
        return 1;
    }

    cout << "Input data checked" << endl;
    cout << "There is no arbitrage" << endl << endl;

    return 0;
}

int main()                                                  ❹
{
    double S0,U,D,R;

    if (GetInputData(S0,U,D,R)==1) return 1;                ❺

    //compute risk-neutral probability
    cout << "q = " << RiskNeutProb(U,D,R) << endl;          ❻

    //compute stock price at node n=3,i=2
    int n=3; int i=2;
    cout << "n = " << n << endl;
    cout << "i = " << i << endl;
    cout << "S(n,i) = " << S(S0,U,D,n,i) << endl;           ❼

    return 0;
}
```

The program works almost exactly as before, but much of the code has been moved into functions. Here is a breakdown of the new features.

❶ `double RiskNeutProb(double U, double D, double R)`
tells the compiler that we are defining a **function** `RiskNeutProb()` that takes three arguments of type `double` and returns a value of type `double`. The body of this function, enclosed within curly brackets, consists of a single line
`return (R-D)/(U-D);`
which computes the value of the expression and returns it to whatever part of the program is going to call this function.

When we need to compute the risk-neutral probability, we can write `RiskNeutProb(U,D,R)` instead of `(R-D)/(U-D)`. It will hardly save us any typing, but a meaningful name for the function improves readability. Moreover, if we decide to change anything in the expression, perhaps to fix a bug, to improve efficiency or to add some extra functionality, we can do it all in one place, which can be very useful if the risk-neutral probability needs to be evaluated in several different places in the code.

❷ The next function

```
double S(double S0, double U, double D, int n, int i)
```

is similar. It takes three arguments of type `double` and two of type `int`, and returns a value of type `double`, computed using the appropriate formula for the stock price at a given node.

When an argument is passed to a function as above, for example as in `double S0`, it is said to be **passed by value**. It is important to understand what happens in this case. When the function is called, a copy of that variable is made in a separate location in computer memory. The function can see and change the copy, but has no access to the original variable. On the other hand, the calling program cannot see the copy (which is in fact destroyed when the function returns control to the calling program) and only has access to the original variable.

In many situations it is important to know that a function has not altered, perhaps inadvertently, the original value of a variable passed to it. For example, it would not do if the function `RiskNeutProb()` inadvertently changed the value of `U`, which is then used again elsewhere in the program to compute the stock price. Passing a parameter by value guarantees that this cannot happen. On the other hand, making copies of variables consumes time, possibly a consideration when calls to the same function are made a large number of times.

❸ When defining a function to handle input data we face a problem because a function in C++ can return only a single value, but we want to enter four numbers as inputs, and the function will need to pass all of them to the program. To deal with this, in

```
int GetInputData(double& S0,
            double& U, double& D, double& R)
```

the arguments are **passed by reference**, which is indicated by `&`. In this case a single copy of the variable in computer memory is shared by the function and the calling program. The function can see and alter the shared variable. Any changes made by the function to this variable remain available to the calling program when the function returns control. This is exactly what we need to pass on the values of the input data.

There is an older and now much out of favour method of achieving a similar result by passing a pointer to a variable. It will be covered in Section 1.6.

The code for inputting and verifying data is largely the same as in Listing 1.2, but now it is placed inside the function. In addition, the function returns a value of type int, which is used to indicate to the calling program whether or not inputting data has been successful.

❹ The body of main() has been streamlined and made more readable. Much of the code has been moved into functions and replaced by calls to these functions:

❺ if (GetInputData(S0,U,D,R)==1) return 1; takes care of inputting and verifying the data, checks if this has been successful, and terminates the program if not.

Note that == is the **logical equality operator**, returning a true value if the expressions on either side are equal, and false otherwise. Do not confuse it with =, the **assignment operator**.

❻ RiskNeutProb(U,D,R) computes the risk-neutral probability.

❼ S(S0,U,D,n,i) computes the stock price at the given node.

Incidentally, int main() indicates that main() is also a function, which returns a value of type int and takes no arguments, as shown by the empty brackets ().

Exercise 1.2 Write a function called interchange() that interchanges the contents of two variables of type double, which are to be passed to the function by reference.

1.4   Separate compilation

If the program uses several functions, which may also be used by other programs, it is advisable to place the functions into a separate file, which is what we do next.

Listing 1.4   BinModel01.cpp

```
#include <iostream>
#include <cmath>
using namespace std;

double RiskNeutProb(double U, double D, double R)
{
    return (R-D)/(U-D);
}
```

```
double S(double S0, double U, double D, int n, int i)
{
   return S0*pow(1+U,i)*pow(1+D,n-i);
}

int GetInputData(double& S0,
                 double& U, double& D, double& R)
{
   //entering data
   cout << "Enter S0: "; cin >> S0;
   cout << "Enter U:  "; cin >> U;
   cout << "Enter D:  "; cin >> D;
   cout << "Enter R:  "; cin >> R;
   cout << endl;

   //making sure that 0<S0, -1<D<U, -1<R
   if (S0<=0.0 || U<=-1.0 || D<=-1.0 || U<=D
                                    || R<=-1.0)
   {
       cout << "Illegal data ranges" << endl;
       cout << "Terminating program" << endl;
       return 1;
   }

  //checking for arbitrage
   if (R>=U || R<=D)
   {
       cout << "Arbitrage exists" << endl;
       cout << "Terminating program" << endl;
       return 1;
   }

   cout << "Input data checked" << endl;
   cout << "There is no arbitrage" << endl << endl;

   return 0;
}
```

The main file is then considerably slimmed down.

Listing 1.5   Main04.cpp

❶

```
#include "BinModel01.h"
#include <iostream>
#include <cmath>
using namespace std;
```

```
int main()
{
   double S0,U,D,R;

   if (GetInputData(S0,U,D,R)==1) return 1;

   //compute risk-neutral probability
   cout << "q = " << RiskNeutProb(U,D,R) << endl;

   //compute stock price at node n=3,i=2
   int n=3; int i=2;
   cout << "n = " << n << endl;
   cout << "i = " << i << endl;
   cout << "S(n,i) = " << S(S0,U,D,n,i) << endl;

   return 0;
}
```

One important point here requires attention.

❶ The compiler will need to know the type of the functions called inside
  `main()`, but these functions are no longer defined in `Main04.cpp`. We
  need to create a header file to provide this information, which will be
  loaded by the new line
  ```
  #include "BinModel01.h"
  ```

Listing 1.6   BinModel01.h

```
#ifndef BinModel01_h                                        ❷
#define BinModel01_h                                        ❷

//computing risk-neutral probability
double RiskNeutProb(double U, double D, double R);          ❸

//computing the stock price at node n,i
double S(double S0, double U, double D, int n, int i);      ❸

//inputting, displaying and checking model data
int GetInputData(double& S0,                                ❸
                 double& U, double& D, double& R);

#endif                                                      ❷
```

❷ The lines
  ```
  #ifndef BinModel01_h
  #define BinModel01_h
  ```
  and

```
#endif
```
are here to avoid multiple inclusion of the header file. If the header file has already been included, anything wrapped between these lines will be skipped. This is more relevant in large projects, where it is easy to lose track of what has or has not been included. It is nevertheless a good habit to follow even in small-scale projects in case the code might become part of a larger library at some point in the future.

❸ The remaining lines are **function prototypes**. They contain the information necessary to compile code that makes calls to these functions, but not the actual definitions of the functions themselves.

At this point it is interesting to experiment with compiling the project consisting of these three files. After initial compilation, changes to one of the .cpp files do not require the other file to be recompiled as long as the function prototypes remain unchanged. (Try it!) In large projects this can mean considerable savings in compilation time.

Moreover, separate compilation makes it possible for developers to share or sell libraries consisting of compiled code and the corresponding header files, but not the actual source code.

1.5 CRR pricer

We are ready to include an option pricer. This will be placed in a separate file with its own header file.

Listing 1.7 Options01.h

```
#ifndef Options01_h
#define Options01_h

//inputting and displaying option data
int GetInputData(int& N, double& K);                    ❶

//pricing European option
double PriceByCRR(double S0, double U, double D,
                  double R, int N, double K);

//computing call payoff
double CallPayoff(double z, double K);

#endif
```

Here is the file containing the definitions of the functions prototyped in the header file.

Listing 1.8   Options01.cpp

```cpp
#include "Options01.h"                                              ❷
#include "BinModel01.h"
#include <iostream>
#include <cmath>
using namespace std;

int GetInputData(int& N, double& K)
{
   cout << "Enter steps to expiry N: "; cin >> N;
   cout << "Enter strike price K:    "; cin >> K;
   cout << endl;
   return 0;
}

double PriceByCRR(double S0, double U, double D,
                  double R, int N, double K)
{
   double q=RiskNeutProb(U,D,R);
   double Price[N+1];                                               ❸
   for (int i=0; i<=N; i++)                                         ❺
   {
      Price[i]=CallPayoff(S(S0,U,D,N,i),K);                         ❹
   }
   for (int n=N-1; n>=0; n--)                                       ❻
   {
      for (int i=0; i<=n; i++)
      {
         Price[i]=(q*Price[i+1]+(1-q)*Price[i])/(1+R);
      }
   }
   return Price[0];
}

double CallPayoff(double z, double K)
{
   if (z>K) return z-K;
   return 0.0;
}
```

The files `BinModel01.cpp` and `BinModel01.h` remain unchanged, but we need to make changes in `main()` to take advantage of the code to compute the price of a call option. While doing so, we also take the opportunity to remove some code no longer needed in `main()`.

Listing 1.9 Main05.cpp

```
#include "BinModel01.h"
#include "Options01.h"
#include <iostream>
#include <cmath>
using namespace std;

int main()
{
    double S0,U,D,R;

    if (GetInputData(S0,U,D,R)==1) return 1;

    double K;     //strike price
    int N;        //steps to expiry

    cout << "Enter call option data:" << endl;
    GetInputData(N,K);
    cout << "European call option price = "
         << PriceByCRR(S0,U,D,R,N,K)
         << endl << endl;

    return 0;
}
```

Much of this should be self-explanatory by now, but a few comments are in order.

❶ `GetInputData()` prototyped in `Options01.h` shares the same name with the function in `BinModel01.h` performing a similar task. This is an example of **function overloading**. Rather than having two differently named functions, it is easier to remember that `GetInputData()` will take care of data input in either case. There is no clash because the compiler can tell which version of the function to call by looking at the arguments, four in the case of the binomial model, or just two for the option. Whenever possible use a similar interface to perform similar tasks.

❷ `#include "Options01.h"`
at the beginning of `Options01.cpp` loads the corresponding header file. Why is it needed? It would seem that `Options01.cpp` should

know all there is to know about its own functions. Yet, when we remove this line, the file will not compile. (Try it!) On the other hand, `BinModel01.cpp` does not include its own header file, but compiles without a complaint.

To resolve the mystery, consider this. When the compiler encounters a call to `CallPayoff()` inside the body of `PriceByCRR()`, it will not yet have seen the definition of `CallPayoff()`, which comes later in the file `Options01.cpp`. As a result, it will not know the number, type and order of parameters that `CallPayoff()` expects, nor the type of return it produces. Compilation cannot proceed unless we provide this information. This could be done by moving the definition of `CallPayoff()` before that of `PriceByCRR()`, but including the header file `Options01.h` is the preferred solution.

❸ `double Price[N+1];`

declares an **array** consisting of N+1 variables of type `double`, which occupy a consecutive segment in computer memory.

❹ `Price[i]` refers to item number i in the array.

Bear in mind that numbering starts with i equal to 0 and runs up to and including N. This gives N+1 elements in the array. Great care should be taken that i cannot take a value outside this range. Nasty runtime errors may occur if it does, and the C++ compiler will be unable to catch this kind of problem.

❺ Inside the body of `PriceByCRR()` a **for loop** is used to set the option prices for each node i at time N to be equal to the payoff at that node according to (1.2).

The loop starts with `i=0`, increases i by 1 after each iteration as indicated by `i++` (which has the effect of increasing the value of i by 1), and continues as long as `i<=N`. In each iteration it executes the code inside the body of the loop, enclosed within the curly brackets `{` and `}`.

❻ This is followed by a double loop computing the option prices from (1.3). The outer loop goes backwards through the times n from N-1 to 0 in steps of 1 (`n--` has the effect of decreasing the value of n by 1). The nested inner loop goes through the nodes i from 0 to n in steps of 1.

At each step n we are recycling the storage space in the `Price[]` array, overwriting entries that are no longer needed.

There are other ways of constructing loops. In Exercise 1.3 it is done using `while` instead of `for`.

Exercise 1.3 Rewrite the loops in `PriceByCRR()` in `Options01.cpp` using `while` instead of `for`. You may need to read about the `while` loop from a C++ manual.

Exercise 1.4 Include checking for input data integrity in the `GetInputData()` function in `Options01.cpp`. You want to ensure that $0 < K$ and $0 < N$.

Exercise 1.5 Modify the `PriceByCRR()` function in `Options01.cpp` to compute the time 0 price of a European option using the **Cox–Ross–Rubinstein (CRR) formula**

$$H(0) = \frac{1}{(1+R)^N} \sum_{i=0}^{N} \frac{N!}{i!(N-i)!} q^i (1-q)^{N-i} h(S(N,i)),$$

instead of the iterative procedure (1.2), (1.3).

Exercise 1.6 Bubble sort is a simple sorting algorithm. It puts a given list of numbers $a_1, \ldots, a_N$ into increasing order by successively comparing adjacent elements and interchanging them if they are in the wrong order. Here is some pseudo code for this algorithm:

for $i := 1$ **to** $N - 1$
  for $j := 1$ **to** $N - i$
    if $a_j > a_{j+1}$ **then** interchange a_j and a_{j+1}
  end
end

Write a function called `bubblesort()` to implement this algorithm. The function should take an array of numbers of type `double` and the size of the array as arguments and return the result in the same array. Use the `interchange()` function from Exercise 1.2 to interchange two numbers inside the body of `bubblesort()`. If necessary, refer to a C++ manual to read about passing an array to a function.

1.6 Pointers

In this section we explore pointers, and use them to develop an alternative version of the code for the option pricer. The principal aim is to give an overview of pointers in C++. The code itself will not be used later, but it should help to understand function pointers in the next section, and other important applications of pointers further down the line.

A **pointer** is a variable used to store an address in computer memory. In C++ there are many pointer types, depending on the type of data to be held at that address. For example, a pointer called `Ptr` in which to store the address of a variable of type `double` is declared by

```
double* Ptr;
```

Then `*Ptr` can be used to access the value of that variable. For example,

```
*Ptr=1.6
```

means that value `1.6` of type `double` will be stored at the address held (we often say, pointed to) by `Ptr`. We can use `*Ptr` whenever we would normally use a variable of type `double`.

On the other hand, if `x` is a variable of type `double` declared by

```
double x;
```

then `&x` designates the address of `x`, and we can set

```
Ptr=&x;
```

if we want `Ptr` to point to `x` (that is, to hold the address of `x`).

Pointers offer an alternative to passing variables to a function by reference. For example, the `GetInputData()` function from `Options01.h` and `Options01.cpp` can be altered as follows:

Listing 1.10 Options02.h

```
#ifndef Options02_h
#define Options02_h

//inputting and displaying option data
int GetInputData(int* PtrN, double* PtrK);
```

❶

```
//pricing European option
double PriceByCRR(double S0, double U, double D,
                  double R, int N, double K);

//computing call payoff
double CallPayoff(double z, double K);

#endif
```

Listing 1.11   Options02.cpp

```
#include "Options02.h"
#include "BinModel01.h"
#include <iostream>
#include <cmath>
using namespace std;

int GetInputData(int* PtrN, double* PtrK)                           ❶
{
   cout << "Enter steps to expiry N: "; cin >> *PtrN;               ❷
   cout << "Enter strike price K:    "; cin >> *PtrK;
   cout << endl;
   return 0;
}

double PriceByCRR(double S0, double U, double D,
                  double R, int N, double K)
{
   double q=RiskNeutProb(U,D,R);
   double Price[N+1];
   for (int i=0; i<=N; i++)
   {
      *(Price+i)=CallPayoff(S(S0,U,D,N,i),K);                       ❹
   }
   for (int n=N-1; n>=0; n--)
   {
      for (int i=0; i<=n; i++)
      {
         *(Price+i)=(q*(*(Price+i+1))+(1-q)*(*(Price+i)))/(1+R);
      }
   }
   return *Price;
}
```

```
double CallPayoff(double z, double K)
{
    if (z>K) return z-K;
    return 0.0;
}
```

To use these changes, we need to make some alterations in `main()`.

Listing 1.12   Main06.cpp

```
#include "BinModel01.h"
#include "Options02.h"
#include <iostream>
#include <cmath>
using namespace std;

int main()
{
    double S0,U,D,R;

    if (GetInputData(S0,U,D,R)==1) return 1;

    double K;     //strike price
    int N;        //steps to expiry

    cout << "Enter call option data:" << endl;
    GetInputData(&N,&K);                                    ❸
    cout << "European call option price = "
         << PriceByCRR(S0,U,D,R,N,K)
         << endl << endl;

    return 0;
}
```

❶ Pointers called `PtrN` and `PtrK` have replaced the variables `N` and `K` that were passed by reference to `GetInputData()`.

❷ `*PtrN` and `*PtrK` are used instead of `N` and `K` in the body of the function `GetInputData()`.

❸ In `main()` the addresses `&N` and `&K` rather than `N` and `K` themselves are passed to `GetInputData()`.

   The effect will be just like in the case of variables passed by reference: `N` and `K` will retain the values obtained by `GetInputData()` after the function has finished its job.

❹ Additionally, this code fragment highlights a connection between arrays and pointers. Here `Price[]` has been declared an array of type `double`. In that case `Price` (without the square brackets `[` and `]`) is a pointer of type `double`. It points to the address of the initial element of the array. That is, `Price` holds the address of `Price[0]`, and we can, in fact, write `*Price` instead of `Price[0]`. Moreover, `Price+i` gives the address of `Price[i]`, and we can write `*(Price+i)` instead of `Price[i]`, as in the code fragment in question.

Exercise 1.7 Modify the `interchange()` function from Exercise 1.2 so that it now takes pointers to two variables of type `double` as parameters instead of having the variables passed by reference.

What changes need to be made in the code for `bubblesort()` in Exercise 1.6 in order to use the modified `interchange()` function?

Exercise 1.8 Modify the function `GetInputData()` from `BinModel01.h` and `BinModel01.cpp` to have the parameters passed to it by pointers rather than by reference. What changes are needed in `Main04.cpp` to call the modified function?

1.7 Function pointers

The option pricer has been hardwired to price calls, but we want to handle other kinds of options such as puts, and ideally to have the ability to add more payoff functions as the need arises without interfering more than absolutely necessary with existing code.

We can readily copy, rename and modify the `CallPayoff()` function to produce a different kind of payoff. For example, see the code for the `PutPayoff()` function in Listings 1.13 and 1.14 below.

We need to call this new payoff function from `PriceByCRR()`. If we just replaced `CallPayoff()` by `PutPayoff()` in the body of `PriceByCRR()`, we would lose the ability to price calls. As an alternative, we could copy, rename and modify `PriceByCRR()` to call the `PutPayoff()` function. This way we would be able to price puts while retaining the ability to price calls. But it is not a neat solution either. If we want to modify `PriceByCRR()` in the future, we would have several copies of it to worry about, one for each option payoff, a potential maintenance nightmare.

What we want is the ability to add new payoff functions without having to retouch the definition of `PriceByCRR()`. Function pointers offer a way to achieve this.

Listing 1.13 Options03.h

```
#ifndef Options03_h
#define Options03_h

//inputting and displaying option data
int GetInputData(int& N, double& K);

//pricing European option
double PriceByCRR(double S0, double U, double D,
                  double R, int N, double K,
                  double (*Payoff)(double z, double K));      ❶

//computing call payoff
double CallPayoff(double z, double K);

//computing put payoff
double PutPayoff(double z, double K);                         ❷

#endif
```

The functions prototyped in this header file are defined next.

Listing 1.14 Options03.cpp

```
#include "Options03.h"
#include "BinModel01.h"
#include <iostream>
#include <cmath>
using namespace std;

int GetInputData(int& N, double& K)
{
    cout << "Enter steps to expiry N: "; cin >> N;
    cout << "Enter strike price K:    "; cin >> K;
    cout << endl;
    return 0;
}

double PriceByCRR(double S0, double U, double D,
                  double R, int N, double K,
                  double (*Payoff)(double z, double K))       ❶
```

```
{
   double q=RiskNeutProb(U,D,R);
   double Price[N+1];
   for (int i=0; i<=N; i++)
   {
      Price[i]=Payoff(S(S0,U,D,N,i),K);
   }
   for (int n=N-1; n>=0; n--)
   {
      for (int i=0; i<=n; i++)
      {
         Price[i]=(q*Price[i+1]+(1-q)*Price[i])/(1+R);
      }
   }
   return Price[0];
}

double CallPayoff(double z, double K)
{
   if (z>K) return z-K;
   return 0.0;
}

double PutPayoff(double z, double K)
{
   if (z<K) return K-z;
   return 0.0;
}
```

Let us put this to work to price both a call and a put.

Listing 1.15   Main07.cpp

```
#include "BinModel01.h"
#include "Options03.h"
#include <iostream>
#include <cmath>
using namespace std;

int main()
{
   double S0,U,D,R;

   if (GetInputData(S0,U,D,R)==1) return 1;

   double K;     //strike price
   int N;        //steps to expiry
```

```
    cout << "Enter call option data:" << endl;
    GetInputData(N,K);
    cout << "European call option price = "
         << PriceByCRR(S0,U,D,R,N,K,CallPayoff)          ❹
         << endl << endl;

    cout << "Enter put option data:" << endl;
    GetInputData(N,K);
    cout << "European put option price =  "
         << PriceByCRR(S0,U,D,R,N,K,PutPayoff)           ❹
         << endl << endl;

    return 0;
}
```

The new features are:

❶ `PriceByCRR()` takes an extra argument, a **function pointer**
`double (*Payoff)(double z, double K)`
A function is stored as a block of code, which can be identified by its address in computer memory. A pointer to a function is a variable type that can hold the address of such a block of memory.

   The expression declaring a function pointer can look somewhat complicated, but it is necessary because the compiler needs to know the type of the function pointed to. That is, it needs to know the number, type and order of the arguments, and the type of the value returned by the function. Here `Payoff` is declared to be a pointer to a function taking two arguments of type `double` and returning a value of type `double`.

❷ A new function `PutPayoff()` is added in `Options03.cpp` and its prototype in the corresponding header file.

❸ `CallPayoff()` in the body of the `PriceByCRR()` function is replaced by `Payoff()`. At compilation time it is therefore unknown which function will actually be called. It is just the type of the function to be called that is known to the compiler. At run time, once a pointer to a function (such as a pointer to `CallPayoff()` or to `PutPayoff()`) is passed to `PriceByCRR()`, the program will know which of these functions to call.

❹ In `Main07.cpp` the function `PriceByCRR()` is called with the pointer `CallPayoff` to the function `CallPayoff()` passed to it to compute the call price, and then called again with the pointer `PutPayoff` to the function `PutPayoff()` to compute the put price.

A pointer to a function has the same name as the function, without the brackets ().

Adding more payoff functions, for example, digital calls or digital puts is now straightforward and involves no changes to existing code. We do this in Exercises 1.9 and 1.10.

Exercise 1.9 The payoff of a **digital call** with strike price K is

$$h^{\text{digit call}}(z) = \begin{cases} 1 & \text{if } K < z, \\ 0 & \text{otherwise.} \end{cases}$$

Include the ability to price digital calls in the program developed in the present section by adding the new payoff function to the file Options03.cpp, just as was done for calls and puts, and suitably modifying the code in Options03.h and Main07.cpp to compute the prices of a digital call option.

Even more interestingly, the code for the new payoff can be placed in a separate .cpp file complete with its own header file, without changing anything at all inside the existing files (other than the main file, which obviously we have to edit to use the new payoffs). This is done in Exercise 1.10. It appears that we have accomplished a lot more than we set out to do in the first place!

Exercise 1.10 The payoff of a **digital put** with strike price K is

$$h^{\text{digit put}}(z) = \begin{cases} 1 & \text{if } K > z, \\ 0 & \text{otherwise.} \end{cases}$$

Add the ability to price digital puts to the program developed in the present section by placing any new code in a separate .cpp file, complete with its own header file, without altering anything at all in the original files, except for the appropriate changes in Main07.cpp.

The scope for introducing errors in existing code is massively reduced while the scope for productive collaboration is increased. Imagine that you are assigned an assistant to develop code to price several new option payoffs. The last thing you want is to let the assistant alter your existing tried and tested code. It would be much more trouble than help if you then had to understand all the changes to your code, and worse if the assistant inadvertently introduced some bugs. But the assistant can in fact work on the new payoffs without even opening your files. All the assistant needs to know is the type of the function that computes option payoffs, which can be found in the header file, and not the inner workings of your code inside the .cpp files.

1.8 Taking stock

We have reached an important milestone and need to stop for a moment to take stock.

The code runs efficiently and meets our objectives. More than that, it is expandable. Further option payoffs can be added as the need arises, without interfering with existing code.

All the same, in practice one would need to include much more functionality in the program. Here is a brief 'to do' list:

- Price a double-digital option.
- Include American options.
- How about path-dependent options? A barrier option? An Asian option?
- Compute the hedging portfolio on top of the price.
- Compute the price from the Black–Scholes formula.
- Approximate the Black–Scholes price by the CRR price.
- Include a Monte Carlo pricer.

We can readily come up with an ad hoc solution to each one of these requests, but things might become messy rapidly when trying to satisfy all of them. We need a design strategy to take care of this kind of complexity in managing and evolving larger projects.

Function pointers gave us a flavour of what can be done, but they do have their limitations. Take the first task on the list, for example. A **double-digital option** does not have a single strike price. It has two parameters, $K_1 < K_2$, the payoff function being

$$h^{\text{double-digit}}(z) = \begin{cases} 1 & \text{if } K_1 < z < K_2, \\ 0 & \text{otherwise.} \end{cases}$$

A function to compute the double-digital payoff would need three arguments, the stock price S and the two parameters K_1, K_2. But our function pointer `Payoff` allows only two arguments.

Various ad hoc measures can be devised to deal with the impasse. One could, for example, redesign the code to take an array of numbers as an argument, so we could pass as many parameters as needed via a single array. This is covered in Exercise 1.11. All we have done so far, including this ad hoc measure, belongs to what is known as the **procedural** style of programming. But there is a much more powerful way, called **object-oriented** programming, to handle increasing complexity in a project. At the heart of it lies the notion of a class, and this is what we are going to use in the next chapter.

Exercise 1.11 Modify the function pointer `Payoff` in `Options03.cpp` so that the function pointed to will accept an array of type `double` in place of the single variable of type `double` that was used to pass the strike price.

Modify the payoff functions `CallPayoff()` and `PutPayoff()` for calls and puts to use with the new function pointer, and modify any remaining code as necessary to work with these.

Take advantage of this new function pointer to include the ability to price double-digital options.

2

Binomial pricer revisited

2.1 Our first class

We want to encapsulate the binomial model consisting of stock and a money market account, while leaving out anything related to options. In C++ this can be achieved using a class, which will include the variables S0, U, D, R determining the binomial model, and also all the functions specific to the model such as RiskNeutProb(). Indeed everything that we have already placed in the files BinModel01.h and BinModel01.cpp will become part of the class.

Listing 2.1 BinModel02.h

```
#ifndef BinModel02_h
#define BinModel02_h

class BinModel                                          ❶
{
    private:
        double S0;                                      ❷
        double U;
        double D;
        double R;
```

```
    public:
        //computing risk-neutral probability
        double RiskNeutProb();                          ❸

        //computing the stock price at node n,i
        double S(int n, int i);                         ❹

        //inputting, displaying and checking model data
        int GetInputData();

        double GetR();                                  ❺
};

#endif
```

Let us examine this new header file, paying attention to links with the previous version of the code.

❶ `class BinModel`

tells the compiler that a **class** named `BinModel` is to be defined. This is followed by the body of the definition enclosed in curly brackets `{` and `}` and a semicolon `;` right behind the closing bracket. (It does not pay to forget the semicolon.)

Inside the curly brackets there is a list of **class members**, such as variables and functions, grouped into `private` and `public` members.

❷ The familiar variables S0, U, D, R are declared here, while their old declarations are going to disappear from `main()`; see Listing 2.5. From now on these variables will live together inside the class. In fact, being listed as **private members** of the class, they will be inaccessible on their own outside this class. Instead, `main()` and other parts of the program will only be able to access them via this class. This makes a lot of sense because the variables really do belong together. They are exactly what it takes to determine the binomial model.

❸ Further down the list of class members there are the declarations of some familiar functions such as `RiskNeutProb()`. They are listed as **public members** of the class, meaning that they will be accessible outside the class. We shall see calls to these functions made from other parts of the program.

There is, however, something unnerving here: S0, U, D, R are left out of the lists of parameters to be passed to these familiar functions. For example, in the line

```
double RiskNeutProb();
```
there is just a set of empty brackets (). How is `RiskNeutProb()` going to compute what it needs to compute if we do not seem to be passing anything to it? It needs to know `U`, `D`, `R` to compute the risk-neutral probability. But in fact it does know these because it is a member of the same class.

Every member function has access to the variables specified as members of the class and knows their declarations given within that class.

❹ On the other hand, we still need to pass non-member parameters explicitly, hence we have
```
double S(int n, int i);
```

❺ A new function `GetR()` has been included so that code outside of the class can obtain the value of `R`. As a `private` member of the class, `R` would otherwise be invisible to the option pricer, but it will be needed for discounting. The function `GetR()`, being a member of the class, can be used to look up the value of `R` and return it to any part of the program that might need this value. The function itself is made `public` so that it can be called from outside the class.

What have we gained by this? The value of `R` can now be looked up but cannot be changed from outside the class. If we did not care that the value of `R` could be changed by some code spreading anarchy outside the class, then we could simply make `R` a `public` member and dispose of `GetR()`. However, this would be risky design, not to be recommended.

There are no similar get functions for `S0`, `U` or `D` because we do not expect these variables to be needed on their own outside the class.

Although in the `BinModel` class all variables are `private` and all functions are `public`, it does not have to be so. If desired, some or all variables can be declared as `public`, so they are accessible (that is, the values stored in them can be seen and changed) from anywhere in the program, and some or all functions can be made `private`, so that they can only be called by members of the class.

In addition to `private` and `public` members, a class may also contain `protected` members, but we shall not be covering these here. Refer to a C++ manual if interested in the vagaries of `protected` members.

When defining a class we do not only make a list of declared members, but also exercise tight control over access rights to those members. A useful rule of thumb (to be readily broken when there is a good reason) is to make all functions in a class `public` and all variables `private`, complete with the accompanying get functions to pass values outside the class when needed. This is exactly what we have done in the `BinModel` class.

Another rule of thumb is that a class should correspond to some real entity. Here the entity is a binomial tree model. The class comprises the data related to the entity (the variables) and the tasks that need to be performed in relation to the entity (the functions).

The next file provides the detailed definitions of the functions declared inside the class.

Listing 2.2   BinModel02.cpp

```
#include "BinModel02.h"
#include <iostream>
#include <cmath>
using namespace std;

double BinModel::RiskNeutProb()                                    ❶
{
    return (R-D)/(U-D);                                            ❷
}

double BinModel::S(int n, int i)                                   ❶
{
    return S0*pow(1+U,i)*pow(1+D,n-i);                            ❷
}

int BinModel::GetInputData()                                       ❶
{
    //entering data
    cout << "Enter S0: "; cin >> S0;                              ❷
    cout << "Enter U:  "; cin >> U;
    cout << "Enter D:  "; cin >> D;
    cout << "Enter R:  "; cin >> R;
    cout << endl;

    //making sure that 0<S0, -1<D<U, -1<R
    if (S0<=0.0 || U<=-1.0 || D<=-1.0 || U<=D
                                      || R<=-1.0)
    {
        cout << "Illegal data ranges" << endl;
        cout << "Terminating program" << endl;
        return 1;
    }

    //checking for arbitrage
    if (R>=U || R<=D)
    {
```

```
        cout << "Arbitrage exists" << endl;
        cout << "Terminating program" << endl;
        return 1;
    }

    cout << "Input data checked" << endl;
    cout << "There is no arbitrage" << endl << endl;

    return 0;
}

double BinModel::GetR()                                    ❶
{
    return R;                                              ❷
}
```

There is very little change to these functions compared with the previous
versions.

❶ The first line of the definition of each function has changed to indicate
that the function is a member of the BinModel class, for example,
double BinModel::RiskNeutProb()
   Like in the header file, there are no declarations of parameters passed
to any member function whenever the parameters are members of the
class.

❷ Nonetheless, these parameters S0, U, D, R do make an appearance inside
the body of each of these functions. The function knows the type of
these parameters and can access their values because they belong to the
same class.

This ends the specifications of the BinModel class. Next we introduce
changes in the remaining code wherever the functions or variables now
included in the class are used.

Listing 2.3   Options04.h

```
#ifndef Options04_h
#define Options04_h

#include "BinModel02.h"

//inputting and displaying option data
int GetInputData(int& N, double& K);
```

```
//pricing European option
double PriceByCRR(BinModel Model, int N, double K,               ❶
                double (*Payoff)(double z, double K));

//computing call payoff
double CallPayoff(double z, double K);

//computing put payoff
double PutPayoff(double z, double K);

#endif
```

The changes affect only one function, namely `PriceByCRR()`.

❶ A single **object** of class `BinModel` is passed to the function instead
of the four variables `S0`, `U`, `D`, `R` of type `double`. An object of class
`BinModel` contains four such variables, so the effect is similar.

`BinModel Model` in the declaration of the `PriceByCRR()` function
means that `Model` is an object of class `BinModel`, just as `int N` indicates that `N` is a variable of type `int`.

In that sense classes can be regarded as an extension of variable types. In
addition to variables of type `double`, `int` or other types available in C++,
we are able to construct compound types by using classes.

Listing 2.4   Options04.cpp

```
#include "Options04.h"
#include "BinModel02.h"
#include <iostream>
#include <cmath>
using namespace std;

int GetInputData(int& N, double& K)
{
   cout << "Enter steps to expiry N: "; cin >> N;
   cout << "Enter strike price K:    "; cin >> K;
   cout << endl;
   return 0;
}

double PriceByCRR(BinModel Model, int N, double K,
                double (*Payoff)(double z, double K))
{
```

```
    double q=Model.RiskNeutProb();                          ❶
    double Price[N+1];
    for (int i=0; i<=N; i++)
    {
        Price[i]=Payoff(Model.S(N,i),K);                    ❷
    }
    for (int n=N-1; n>=0; n--)
    {
        for (int i=0; i<=n; i++)
        {
            Price[i]=(q*Price[i+1]+(1-q)*Price[i])
                /(1+Model.GetR());                          ❸
        }
    }
    return Price[0];
}

double CallPayoff(double z, double K)
{
    if (z>K) return z-K;
    return 0.0;
}

double PutPayoff(double z, double K)
{
    if (z<K) return K-z;
    return 0.0;
}
```

As in the header file, all changes are found in the `PriceByCRR()` function.

❶ `Model.RiskNeutProb()` computes the risk-neutral probability. Because `Model` is an object of class `BinModel`, it contains its own variables `U`, `D`, `R`. The `RiskNeutProb()` function defined within this class is called with these variables implicitly passed to it via the object `Model`.

   When a function that is a member of a class is called outside the class, then its name should be preceded by an object of that class and the **dot operator**.

❷ Similar remarks apply to `Model.S(N,n)`.

❸ Note the call to `Model.GetR()` to fetch the value of `R` belonging to `Model`. We need to do it this way because `R` is a `private` member of the class.

   Had we made `R` a public member of the `BinModel` class, we would have been able to access it directly by `Model.R` from outside the class, without a need for the `GetR()` function. (Try it!) We have already discussed the perils of such an approach, however.

Listing 2.5 Main08.cpp

```cpp
#include "BinModel02.h"
#include "Options04.h"
#include <iostream>
#include <cmath>
using namespace std;

int main()
{
    BinModel Model;                                              ❶

    if (Model.GetInputData()==1) return 1;                       ❷

    double K;    //strike price
    int N;       //steps to expiry

    cout << "Enter call option data:" << endl;
    GetInputData(N,K);
    cout << "European call option price = "
         << PriceByCRR(Model,N,K,CallPayoff)                     ❸
         << endl << endl;

    cout << "Enter put option data:" << endl;
    GetInputData(N,K);
    cout << "European put option price =  "
         << PriceByCRR(Model,N,K,PutPayoff)                      ❸
         << endl << endl;

    return 0;
}
```

Some comments are needed to explain the goings-on inside `main()`.

❶ `BinModel Model;`
   declares `Model` to be an object of class `BinModel`.

❷ `Model.GetInputData()`
   takes care of inputting four numbers and assigns them to the variables `S0`, `U`, `D`, `R` inside the object `Model`.

❸ `PriceByCRR(Model,N,K,CallPayoff)`
   and
   `PriceByCRR(Model,N,K,PutPayoff)`

have `Model` passed to them as one of the arguments. This amounts to passing the variables `S0`, `U`, `D`, `R` belonging to `Model`.

Having introduced our first class, we are a step closer to reconfiguring the code in the spirit of object-oriented programming. It is time to take the next step.

2.2 Inheritance

The next step will in fact be more of a leap. We want to capture the concept of European options in terms of classes, but this proves more intricate than the binomial model class.

What makes a European option a European option? It should certainly have an expiry date N and a payoff function $h(z)$. However, we do not need to know the concrete form of the payoff function to express the price by the CRR procedure (1.2), (1.3).

On the other hand, there are, for example, European calls or puts, which are European options, and on top of this have a strike price K and a concrete form of the payoff function, namely $h^{\text{call}}(z) = (z-K)^+$ for a call and $h^{\text{put}}(z) = (K-z)^+$ for a put.

Every European call is a European option, but not every European option is a European call. Similar for a put. European options form a wider class than European calls or puts. European calls and European puts are subclasses of European options.

These considerations show how classes and subclasses work in plain language. In C++ this is similar and comes under the name of inheritance. It should now be much easier to figure out what happens in the next header file.

Listing 2.6   Options05.h

```
#ifndef Options05_h
#define Options05_h

#include "BinModel02.h"

class EurOption
{
    private:                                      ❶
        //steps to expiry
```

```
        int N;
        //pointer to payoff function
        double (*Payoff)(double z, double K);
    public:
        void SetN(int N_){N=N_;}
        void SetPayoff
            (double (*Payoff_)(double z, double K))
            {Payoff=Payoff_;}
        //pricing European option
        double PriceByCRR(BinModel Model, double K);
};

//computing call payoff
double CallPayoff(double z, double K);

class Call: public EurOption
{
    private:
        double K; //strike price
    public:
        Call(){SetPayoff(CallPayoff);}
        double GetK(){return K;}
        int GetInputData();
};

//computing put payoff
double PutPayoff(double z, double K);

class Put: public EurOption
{
    private:
        double K; //strike price
    public:
        Put(){SetPayoff(PutPayoff);}
        double GetK(){return K;}
        int GetInputData();
};

#endif
```

We need to work through this file in some detail.

❶ The EurOption class is defined first with two private variables:

  ❷ N of type int to hold the number of steps to expiry date.

  ❸ Payoff, a pointer to a function that takes two arguments of type double and returns a value of type double. It will be used as a pointer to the payoff function. The payoff function itself is not

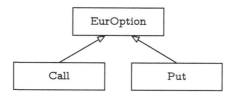

Figure 2.1 Inheritance relationships in Listing 2.6.

defined within this class, in line with the idea that the `EurOption` class should cater for an arbitrary payoff.

❹ There are three `public` functions belonging to the `EurOption` class:

    ❺ `SetN()`, which will be used when the number of steps to expiry date is read from the keyboard and needs to be passed to an object of class `EurOption`.

       The function `SetN()` does not return a value of any kind, which is indicated by the keyword `void`.

    ❻ `SetPayoff()`, to set the pointer to the payoff function once it is decided which concrete option is to be priced. It is important to understand that this decision can be made at run time and does not have to be cast in stone within the code.

    ❼ `PriceByCRR()`, the option pricer. We have already seen how the pricer can work with a pointer to the payoff function. The only difference here is that the pointer will be passed to the pricer as a member of the same class.

❽ `class Call: public EurOption`
introduces `Call` as a **subclass** of the `EurOption` class. There is also a similar subclass for puts. This defines the inheritance relationships, as represented by Figure 2.1.

    In this context `public` is again about controlling access rights. It means that all `public` members of the class become `public` members of the subclass. It is also possible to introduce `private` subclasses, in which case all `public` members of the class become `private` members of the subclass. The `private` members of a class always become `private` members of a subclass. Once again, we give `protected` members a wide berth.

    As a result, the variables N and `Payoff` belonging to the `EurOption` class become `private` members of the `Call` class, while the functions `SetN()`, `SetPayoff()` and `PriceByCRR()` become public members of the `Call` class.

A point to remember: Even though the private members `Payoff` and `N` of the `EurOption` class become members of the subclass `Call`, the subclass has no access to them. This is in order to protect privacy. Otherwise one would only need to create a subclass to gain access to any `private` member of a class.

⑨ Declaring `double K;` in the body of the subclass means that, in addition to `N` and `Payoff` inherited from `EurOption`, the `Call` subclass (and similarly the `Put` subclass) comprises one more variable `K`, which will be used to hold the strike price.

⑩ The `Call` class (and similarly the `Put` class) has three more `public` functions in addition to those inherited from `EurOption`:

⑪ `Call(){SetPayoff(CallPayoff);}`
requires a detailed exploration. It has no return type, not even `void`, and has the same name as the class of which it is a member. This indicates that this is a so-called **constructor function** of the class.

Constructor functions are very special in that they are executed automatically whenever an object of the corresponding class is initiated. For example, when an object `Option1` of class `Call` is created in `main()` (see Listing 2.8) by
`Call Option1;`
the constructor function will run behind the scenes and set the function pointer `Payoff` to point to the `CallPayoff()` function. It will save us the hassle of having to do this explicitly.

Another noteworthy feature is that the full definition of the `Call()` function rather than just its prototype is given in the header file. It is customary to do so if the definition is short. (As an aside, there is also a technical aspect concerning the way a function defined inside the class is compiled; regarding this refer to a C++ manual to read about `inline` functions.)

Similar remarks apply to the constructor function for the `Put` class.

⑫ `GetK()` will allow code outside the class to look up the value of the new `private` variable `K`.

⑬ `GetInputData()` is self-explanatory.

Note that the same name is used as for the function belonging to the `BinModel` class responsible for inputting data. This is yet another example of function overloading. There is no clash because these functions are members of different classes. The compiler will know which one to run in any given context.

The next file defines those functions that have been declared but not defined in the header file.

Listing 2.7 Options05.cpp

```
#include "Options05.h"
#include "BinModel02.h"
#include <iostream>
#include <cmath>
using namespace std;

double EurOption::PriceByCRR(BinModel Model, double K)
{
   double q=Model.RiskNeutProb();
   double Price[N+1];
   for (int i=0; i<=N; i++)
   {
      Price[i]=Payoff(Model.S(N,i),K);
   }
   for (int n=N-1; n>=0; n--)
   {
      for (int i=0; i<=n; i++)
      {
         Price[i]=(q*Price[i+1]+(1-q)*Price[i])
            /(1+Model.GetR());
      }
   }
   return Price[0];
}

double CallPayoff(double z, double K)
{
   if (z>K) return z-K;
   return 0.0;
}

int Call::GetInputData()
{
   cout << "Enter call option data:" << endl;
   int N;
   cout << "Enter steps to expiry N: "; cin >> N;
   SetN(N);
   cout << "Enter strike price K:    "; cin >> K;
   cout << endl;
   return 0;
}

double PutPayoff(double z, double K)
{
```

```
      if (z<K) return K-z;
      return 0.0;
}

int Put::GetInputData()
{
   cout << "Enter put option data:" << endl;
   int N;
   cout << "Enter steps to expiry N: "; cin >> N;
   SetN(N);                                                  ❶
   cout << "Enter strike price K:    "; cin >> K;
   cout << endl;
   return 0;
}
```

There is very little new or particularly exciting here. Just one point to note.

❶ In GetInputData() we have to work a little bit harder to set the value of N compared with K. This is because N is a variable inherited from the EurOption class, declared as private in that class. As a result, the subclasses do not have direct access to it and have to use the SetN() function belonging to the EurOption class. Meanwhile, K is a variable defined within the subclasses Call and Put, which therefore have direct access to it.

We are ready to proceed to the file containing the main() function, which conducts the workflow.

Listing 2.8 Main09.cpp

```
#include "BinModel02.h"
#include "Options05.h"
#include <iostream>
#include <cmath>
using namespace std;

int main()
{
   BinModel Model;

   if (Model.GetInputData()==1) return 1;

   Call Option1;
   Option1.GetInputData();                                   ❶
   cout << "European call option price = "
```

```
        << Option1.PriceByCRR(Model,Option1.GetK())      ❷
        << endl << endl;

    Put Option2;
    Option2.GetInputData();                              ❶
    cout << "European put option price = "
        << Option2.PriceByCRR(Model,Option2.GetK())      ❷
        << endl << endl;

    return 0;
}
```

It should not be hard to understand what this program does, so let us em-
phasise just a couple of things.

❶ Since `Option1` is a `Call`, and `Option2` is a `Put`, it is clear which
version of the `GetInputData()` function is to be executed by
`Option1.GetInputData();`
and, respectively, by
`Option2.GetInputData();`

❷ The same applies to the `PriceByCRR()` and `GetK()` functions.

The effort we have invested in setting up the classes is beginning to pay
off, resulting in streamlined code within `main()`. It is possible to extend
the functionality by adding further kinds of options, for example digital
calls or digital puts, as long as the payoff depends only on one parameter.

One signal that there is room for better design is that the `EurOption`
class contains references to the strike price variable `K`. This should not be
the case because, in fact, not every European option has a strike price in
the first place. There are options whose payoff depends on two parameters rather than a single strike price, for example a double-digital option, a
bull spread or a bear spread. Other payoff functions may have even more
parameters.

If we want to extend the code to include payoffs that take a different
number of parameters, we have almost reached the limit of what pointers
to functions can naturally do. It is certainly possible to accomplish more
with pointers, but the code might grow complicated.

Generally, pointers to functions do not sit too comfortably together with
object-oriented programming, even though they can still prove useful some-
times. The time has come to call upon virtual functions to replace pointers
to functions in our code. This is what will happen in the next section.

Exercise 2.1 A definite integral can be computed numerically by the trapezoidal approximation

$$\int_a^b f(x)dx \approx \frac{h}{2}\left(f(x_0) + 2f(x_1) + \cdots + 2f(x_{N-1}) + f(x_N)\right),$$

where $h = \frac{b-a}{N}$ and where $x_n = a + nh$ for $n = 0, 1, \ldots, N$. Write a class called DefInt to compute the trapezoidal approximation of $\int_a^b f(x)dx$ for a given function f. The class should contain the following:

(1) Private members to hold the values of the integration limits a, b and a pointer to the function f.

(2) A constructor function such that the integration limits a, b and the pointer to the function f can be initiated at the time of creating an object of the class like this:
    DefInt MyInt(a,b,f);

(3) A public function ByTrapezoid() taking N as an argument and returning the trapezoidal approximation to the integral when called by
    MyInt.Trapezoidal(N);

(4) You may also want to include another public function BySimpson() to compute the Simpson approximation to the integral (look it up in literature).

2.3 Virtual functions

Without more ado, we list the code, and then we work our way through it.

Listing 2.9 Options06.h

```
#ifndef Options06_h
#define Options06_h

#include "BinModel02.h"

class EurOption                                         ❶
{
    private:
```

```
      int N; //steps to expiry
   public:
      void SetN(int N_){N=N_;}
      //Payoff defined to return 0.0
      //for pedagogical purposes.
      //To use a pure virtual function replace by
      //virtual double Payoff(double z)=0;
      virtual double Payoff(double z){return 0.0;}
      //pricing European option
      double PriceByCRR(BinModel Model);
};

class Call: public EurOption
{
   private:
      double K; //strike price
   public:
      void SetK(double K_){K=K_;}
      int GetInputData();
      double Payoff(double z);
};

class Put: public EurOption
{
   private:
      double K; //strike price
   public:
      void SetK(double K_){K=K_;}
      int GetInputData();
      double Payoff(double z);
};

#endif
```

Listing 2.10 Options06.cpp

```
#include "Options06.h"
#include "BinModel02.h"
#include <iostream>
#include <cmath>
using namespace std;

double EurOption::PriceByCRR(BinModel Model)
{
   double q=Model.RiskNeutProb();
   double Price[N+1];
   for (int i=0; i<=N; i++)
```

```
      {
         Price[i]=Payoff(Model.S(N,i));
      }
      for (int n=N-1; n>=0; n--)
      {
         for (int i=0; i<=n; i++)
         {
            Price[i]=(q*Price[i+1]+(1-q)*Price[i])
               /(1+Model.GetR());
         }
      }
      return Price[0];
}

int Call::GetInputData()
{
   cout << "Enter call option data:" << endl;
   int N;
   cout << "Enter steps to expiry N: "; cin >> N;
   SetN(N);
   cout << "Enter strike price K:    "; cin >> K;
   cout << endl;
   return 0;
}

double Call::Payoff(double z)
{
   if (z>K) return z-K;
   return 0.0;
}

int Put::GetInputData()
{
   cout << "Enter put option data:" << endl;
   int N;
   cout << "Enter steps to expiry N: "; cin >> N;
   SetN(N);
   cout << "Enter strike price K:    "; cin >> K;
   cout << endl;
   return 0;
}

double Put::Payoff(double z)
{
   if (z<K) return K-z;
   return 0.0;
}
```

Listing 2.11   Main10.cpp

```
#include "BinModel02.h"
#include "Options06.h"
#include <iostream>
#include <cmath>
using namespace std;

int main()
{
   BinModel Model;

   if (Model.GetInputData()==1) return 1;

   Call Option1;
   Option1.GetInputData();
   cout << "European call option price = "
       << Option1.PriceByCRR(Model)
       << endl << endl;

   Put Option2;
   Option2.GetInputData();
   cout << "European put option price = "
       << Option2.PriceByCRR(Model)
       << endl << endl;

   return 0;
}
```

❻

❼

There are important observations to be made.

❶ The name of the game is clean design. No pointer to a function in sight in the EurOption class. The SetPayoff() function is gone too. There is no pointer to a function to be set anymore.

❷ There are no constructor functions calling SetPayoff() in the Call and Put subclasses either.

❸ It gets even better. The function PriceByCRR() in the EurOption class no longer requires K to be passed. This is how we like it because K has no business to be in this class (see the comments at the end of Section 2.2).

❹ In place of the function pointer Payoff, we now have the Payoff() function defined in the EurOption class by

```
virtual double Payoff(double z){return 0.0;}
```

It is a function accepting an argument of type `double` and returning a `double`. This function does very little by itself. It just returns `0.0`, which is quite useless, except that it might help to explain **virtual functions**. What does `virtual` mean? The mystery will soon be revealed.

⑤ There are also `Payoff()` functions defined in the `Call` and `Put` subclasses, and these will do some useful work. They are actually the old functions `CallPayoff()` and `PutPayoff()`.

To see what happens compile and run the program. The correct put and call prices are computed. The `Payoff()` functions from the `Call` and `Put` subclasses must have been executed in the right places to do their job. Now remove the keyword `virtual`, then compile and run the program again. All option prices are returned as 0. It would appear that the `Payoff()` function from the `EurOption` class was called every time.

How did the program decide which version of `Payoff()` to call when? Being declared as a `virtual` function in the `EurOption` class makes it possible for `Payoff()` to recognise, at run time, when an object of a subclass is passed to it via a pointer to the parent class. The version of `Payoff()` belonging to that subclass is then executed.

Do not panic! Let us go through the workflow of this program. We use call options as an example, but similar comments are applicable to puts.

⑥ `Call Option1;`
in `main()` declares `Option1` to be an object of class `Call`.

⑦ The function `PriceByCRR()` belongs to the `EurOption` class and expects to be called with an object of that class. However, when
`Option1.PriceByCRR(Model)`
is executed, the function is called with `Option1`, in fact an object of the `Call` subclass.

Fortunately, every object of the subclass `Call` can be regarded as an object of the parent class `EurOption`. It is the essence of subclasses. Every European call option is a European option. The `PriceByCRR()` function is therefore happy to work with the object `Option1`. However, as far as it is concerned, this is an object of the `EurOption` class.

❽ When `PriceByCRR()` calls the `Payoff()` function, it passes a pointer to `Option1` behind the scenes. This is where `virtual` works its magic.

With `virtual` removed, `Payoff()` takes it at face value. It has been handed a pointer supposedly to an object of class `EurOption` by the `PriceByCRR()` function, which knows no better. The version of `Payoff()` belonging to the `EurOption` class is therefore executed and returns `0.0`. This is what gave us the wrong option prices.

With `virtual` in place, `Payoff()` becomes smarter. It does its own checking, discovering that it has in fact been past a pointer to an object of class `Call`. The correct version of `Payoff()` belonging to the `Call` class is then executed, and all is well and good.

❾ The `Payoff()` function in the `EurOption` class was defined to return `0.0`. It helped us to understand `virtual` functions, but serves no useful purpose when pricing options. It does no harm, but in a well-designed program it is best to avoid redundant code. This can be accomplished by declaring `Payoff()` in the `EurOption` class by

```
virtual double Payoff(double z)=0;
```

The line is already in the header file `Options06.h`, commented out but ready to use. It will tell the compiler not to look for the definition of `Payoff()` in this class because there is none.

With this new line replacing the old one, the `EurOption` class now has a member function called `Payoff()`, but actually does not know how to run this function. Isn't this just like for a general European option, where we know that there is a payoff function $h(z)$, but do not need to know the actual formula for it when setting up the pricing procedure (1.2), (1.3)?

A `virtual` function with no definition as indicated by `=0` is called a **pure virtual function**, and the class containing it is called an **abstract class**. We have the abstract concept of European option represented by the abstract `EurOption` class!

Bear in mind that when a class contains a pure virtual function, it is impossible to declare an object of that class. The compiler will grind to a halt and complain if you do. (Try it!) Otherwise someone might attempt to call the undefined pure virtual function with such an object, and where would it get them?

Exercise 2.2 Add the ability to price **bull spreads** and **bear spreads** by introducing new subclasses `BullSpread` and `BearSpread` of the `EurOption` class defined in `Options06.h`. Use the new classes, making suitable changes in `Main10.cpp` to price European bull and bear spreads.

The payoffs of a bull spread and a bear spread, which depend on two parameters $K_1 < K_2$, are given by

$$h^{\text{bull}}(z) = \begin{cases} 0 & \text{if } z \leq K_1, \\ z - K_1 & \text{if } K_1 < z < K_2, \\ K_2 - K_1 & \text{if } K_2 \leq z, \end{cases}$$

and

$$h^{\text{bear}}(z) = \begin{cases} K_2 - K_1 & \text{if } z \leq K_1, \\ K_2 - z & \text{if } K_1 < z < K_2, \\ 0 & \text{if } K_2 < z. \end{cases}$$

Exercise 2.3 Rewrite the code for numerical integration in Exercise 2.1 replacing function pointers by virtual functions.

2.4 Summing up

We have come to the end of another important stage. The code has been recast in the style of object-oriented programming. Our classes reflect the relationships between real entities, namely the binomial model and European options of various kinds.

An added bonus is that the program can be expanded without interfering with existing files (other than that containing the `main()` function). As an example, we set up a new class `DoubDigitOpt` to price double-digital options. We managed such options in Exercise 1.11 using arrays and pointers to functions, but now we can produce neater code.

The new class is declared in a separate header file `DoubDigitOpt.h` and defined in the corresponding file `DoubDigitOpt.cpp`.

Listing 2.12 **DoubDigitOpt.h**

```
#ifndef DoubDigitOpt_h
#define DoubDigitOpt_h

#include "Options06.h"

class DoubDigitOpt: public EurOption
{
   private:
      double K1; //parameter 1
      double K2; //parameter 2
   public:
      int GetInputData();
      double Payoff(double z);
};

#endif
```

Listing 2.13 **DoubDigitOpt.cpp**

```
#include "DoubDigitOpt.h"
#include <iostream>
using namespace std;

int DoubDigitOpt::GetInputData()
{
   cout << "Enter double-digital option data:" << endl;
   int N;
   cout << "Enter steps to expiry N: "; cin >> N;
   SetN(N);
   cout << "Enter parameter K1:      "; cin >> K1;
   cout << "Enter parameter K2:      "; cin >> K2;
   cout << endl;
   return 0;
}

double DoubDigitOpt::Payoff(double z)
{
   if (K1<z && z<K2) return 1.0;
   return 0.0;
}
```

To design this new code, all that the programmer really needs to see is the header file Options06.h, but there is no necessity to know the contents of `Options06.cpp` (though it does help to know them and to work by altering existing code).

The new files `DoubDigitOpt.h` and `DoubDigitOpt.cpp` can be added to the existing project. A few extra lines in `main()` will show pricing double-digital options in action:

Listing 2.14 Main11.cpp

```cpp
#include "BinModel02.h"
#include "Options06.h"
#include "DoubDigitOpt.h"
#include <iostream>
#include <cmath>
using namespace std;

int main()
{
   BinModel Model;

   if (Model.GetInputData()==1) return 1;

   Call Option1;
   Option1.GetInputData();
   cout << "European call option price = "
        << Option1.PriceByCRR(Model)
        << endl << endl;

   Put Option2;
   Option2.GetInputData();
   cout << "European put option price = "
        << Option2.PriceByCRR(Model)
        << endl << endl;

   DoubDigitOpt Option3;
   Option3.GetInputData();
   cout << "European double-digital option price = "
        << Option3.PriceByCRR(Model)
        << endl << endl;

   return 0;
}
```

Nothing needs to be changed in the remaining files, and if they have already been compiled, there will be no need to recompile them when we build the project again. (Try it!)

We have a powerful tool for collaboration and managing complex software development projects.

Exercise 2.4   Add further payoffs, namely, **strangle** and **butterfly** spreads, by means of subclasses of the `EurOption` class placed in separate files, without changing anything in existing code, except for the necessary changes in `Main11.cpp`, to price options with the newly introduced payoffs.

The payoffs of strangle and butterfly spreads, which depend on two parameters $K_1 < K_2$, are as follows:

$$h^{\text{strangle}}(z) = \begin{cases} K_1 - z & \text{if } z \leq K_1, \\ 0 & \text{if } K_1 < z \leq K_2, \\ z - K_2 & \text{if } K_2 < z, \end{cases}$$

and

$$h^{\text{butterfly}}(z) = \begin{cases} z - K_1 & \text{if } K_1 < z \leq \frac{K_1 + K_2}{2}, \\ K_2 - z & \text{if } \frac{K_1 + K_2}{2} < z \leq K_2, \\ 0 & \text{otherwise.} \end{cases}$$

3

American options

In addition to pricing European options, we want to include the ability to price American options in the binomial model.

The holder of an **American option** has the right to exercise it at any time up to and including the expiry date N. If the option is exercised at time step n and node i of the binomial tree (1.1), then the holder will receive payoff $h(S(n, i))$.

The price $H(n, i)$ of an American option at any time step n and node i in the binomial tree can be computed by the following procedure, which proceeds by backward induction on n:

- At the expiry date N

$$H(N, i) = h(S(N, i)) \tag{3.1}$$

  for each node $i = 0, 1, \ldots, N$.
- If $H(n+1, i)$ is already known at each node $i = 0, 1, \ldots, n+1$ for some $n = 0, \ldots, N - 1$, then

$$H(n, i) = \max\left(\frac{qH(n + 1, i + 1) + (1 - q)H(n + 1, i)}{1 + R}, h(S(n, i))\right) \tag{3.2}$$

  for each node $i = 0, 1, \ldots, n$.

In particular, $H(0)$ at the root node of the tree is the price of the American option at time 0. Note that the discounted price process $(1 + R)^{-n}H(n, i)$ is the **Snell envelope** of the discounted payoff process $(1 + R)^{-n}h(S(n, i))$. Fore details, see [DMFM].

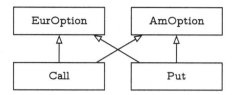

Figure 3.1 Inheritance relationships in Listing 3.1.

3.1 Multiple inheritance

Just as for European options, we can distinguish subclasses of American options according to the payoff, such as puts, calls, digital calls, bull spreads and many others. For now we restrict ourselves to puts and calls.

   In Section 2.2 we saw how to use inheritance in C++ to set up subclasses. A new feature here is that an option with a particular payoff such as a put can be either of European or American type. This can be modelled in C++ by means of multiple inheritance. In addition to the EurOption class, we define a new AmOption class, and make Put a subclass of both the EurOption and AmOption classes. Similarly, Call (and possibly more classes for other payoffs) will also be inheriting from both the EurOption and AmOption classes, as in Figure 3.1. The code to capture this structure follows below.

Listing 3.1   Options07.h

```
#ifndef Options07_h
#define Options07_h

#include "BinModel02.h"

class EurOption
{
   private:
      int N; //steps to expiry
   public:
      void SetN(int N_){N=N_;}
      virtual double Payoff(double z)=0;
      //pricing European option
      double PriceByCRR(BinModel Model);
};

class AmOption
{
```
❶

```
    private:
        int N; //steps to expiry
    public:
        void SetN(int N_){N=N_;}
        virtual double Payoff(double z)=0;
        //pricing American option
        double PriceBySnell(BinModel Model);                    ❷
};

class Call: public EurOption, public AmOption            ❸
{
    private:
        double K; //strike price
    public:
        void SetK(double K_){K=K_;}
        int GetInputData();
        double Payoff(double z);
};

class Put: public EurOption, public AmOption             ❸
{
    private:
        double K; //strike price
    public:
        void SetK(double K_){K=K_;}
        int GetInputData();
        double Payoff(double z);
};

#endif
```

We encounter some new features in this header file.

❶ A new class AmOption is introduced, similar to the EurOption class.

❷ PriceBySnell() in the AmOption class replaces the PriceByCRR() function from the EurOption class.

❸ Because puts and calls can be either of European or American type, the Call and Put classes inherit from both the EurOption and AmOption classes. For example,
class Put: public EurOption, public AmOption
declares Put as a public subclass of the EurOption class as well as of the AmOption class. Similar for the Call class.

The functions belonging to these classes are defined next.

Listing 3.2 Options07.cpp

```cpp
#include "Options07.h"
#include "BinModel02.h"
#include <iostream>
#include <cmath>
#include <vector>
using namespace std;

double EurOption::PriceByCRR(BinModel Model)
{
   double q=Model.RiskNeutProb();
   vector<double> Price(N+1);
   for (int i=0; i<=N; i++)
   {
      Price[i]=Payoff(Model.S(N,i));
   }
   for (int n=N-1; n>=0; n--)
   {
      for (int i=0; i<=n; i++)
      {
         Price[i]=(q*Price[i+1]+(1-q)*Price[i])
            /(1+Model.GetR());
      }
   }
   return Price[0];
}

double AmOption::PriceBySnell(BinModel Model)
{
   double q=Model.RiskNeutProb();
   vector<double> Price(N+1);
   double ContVal;
   for (int i=0; i<=N; i++)
   {
      Price[i]=Payoff(Model.S(N,i));
   }
   for (int n=N-1; n>=0; n--)
   {
      for (int i=0; i<=n; i++)
      {
         ContVal=(q*Price[i+1]+(1-q)*Price[i])
                            /(1+Model.GetR());
         Price[i]=Payoff(Model.S(n,i));
         if (ContVal>Price[i]) Price[i]=ContVal;
      }
   }
   return Price[0];
}
```

```
int Call::GetInputData()
{
   cout << "Enter call option data:" << endl;
   int N;
   cout << "Enter steps to expiry N: "; cin >> N;
   EurOption::SetN(N); AmOption::SetN(N);
   cout << "Enter strike price K:    "; cin >> K;
   cout << endl;
   return 0;
}

double Call::Payoff(double z)
{
   if (z>K) return z-K;
   return 0.0;
}

int Put::GetInputData()
{
   cout << "Enter put option data:" << endl;
   int N;
   cout << "Enter steps to expiry N: "; cin >> N;
   EurOption::SetN(N); AmOption::SetN(N);
   cout << "Enter strike price K:    "; cin >> K;
   cout << endl;
   return 0;
}

double Put::Payoff(double z)
{
   if (z<K) return K-z;
   return 0.0;
}
```

❶ The main new addition is the function `PriceBySnell()` belonging
to the `AmOption` class. The Snell envelope procedure (3.1), (3.2) is
implemented in this function, returning the option price at time 0.

❷ An interesting feature used in the `PriceBySnell()` function (and also
introduced in place of the array in `PriceByCRR()`) is the **vector<>**
template from the **Standard Template Library** (**STL**).

```
#include <vector>
```

loads the appropriate library to make vectors available in the program.

In addition to vectors, the STL contains many other useful predefined
data structures.

❸ `vector<double> Price(N+1);`
declares a vector comprising N+1 variables of type `double`.

❹ Component i of the vector is referred to by `Price[i]` in the code, similar to using an array of type `double`.

❺ The `GetInputData()` function in the `Put` and `Call` classes contains
`EurOption::SetN(N); AmOption::SetN(N);`
to set the value of N in both the `EurOption` and `AmOption` classes.

There are two separate variables N in the `EurOption` and `AmOption` classes, both holding the same value for the expiry date. It is arguably a design flaw since one variable should be sufficient. In Section 3.2 we are going to improve the code so that a single variable N is shared between the two classes.

The pricing of both European and American options is now easily accomplished in `main()`.

Listing 3.3   Main12.cpp

```cpp
#include "BinModel02.h"
#include "Options07.h"
#include <iostream>
using namespace std;

int main()
{
   BinModel Model;

   if (Model.GetInputData()==1) return 1;

   Call Option1;
   Option1.GetInputData();
   cout << "European call option price = "
        << Option1.PriceByCRR(Model)
        << endl;
   cout << "American call option price = "
        << Option1.PriceBySnell(Model)
        << endl << endl;

   Put Option2;
   Option2.GetInputData();
   cout << "European put option price = "
        << Option2.PriceByCRR(Model)
        << endl;
   cout << "American put option price = "
        << Option2.PriceBySnell(Model)
```

```
        << endl << endl;

    return 0;
}
```

3.2 Virtual inheritance

The code developed in Section 3.1 to include American options suffers from a drawback. The EurOption class and the AmOption class each have their own variable N to store the expiry date. In the line
EurOption::SetN(N); AmOption::SetN(N);
the variable N had to be initiated by the same value separately for European and American options. It is redundant to have two copies of the same number. The expiry date is a common feature shared by all options. What we need is a single copy of N shared between the EurOption and AmOption classes.

Similar remarks apply to the function SetN() and the virtual function Payoff(). It would be much more sensible to have a single copy of each of these functions shared between the EurOption and AmOption classes rather than two copies owned separately by each of these two classes.

How do we achieve this? We create a new class, and call it the Option class, to contain the common features shared by all options such as the expiry date and a payoff function. Then we change the EurOption and AmOption classes to become subclasses of the Option class, so they will inherit these features. This is what happens in the next version of the code.

Listing 3.4 Options08.h

```
#ifndef Options08_h
#define Options08_h

#include "BinModel02.h"

class Option
{
    private:
        int N; //steps to expiry
    public:
        void SetN(int N_){N=N_;}
```

```
      int GetN(){return N;}                                    ❹
      virtual double Payoff(double z)=0;
};

class EurOption: public virtual Option                         ❸
{
   public:
      //pricing European option
      double PriceByCRR(BinModel Model);
};

class AmOption: public virtual Option                          ❸
{
   public:
      //pricing American option
      double PriceBySnell(BinModel Model);
};

class Call: public EurOption, public AmOption
{
   private:
      double K; //strike price
   public:
      void SetK(double K_){K=K_;}
      int GetInputData();
      double Payoff(double z);
};

class Put: public EurOption, public AmOption
{
   private:
      double K; //strike price
   public:
      void SetK(double K_){K=K_;}
      int GetInputData();
      double Payoff(double z);
};

#endif
```

Listing 3.5   Options08.cpp

```
#include "Options08.h"
#include "BinModel02.h"
#include <iostream>
#include <cmath>
#include <vector>
```

```
using namespace std;

double EurOption::PriceByCRR(BinModel Model)
{
   double q=Model.RiskNeutProb();
   int N=GetN();
   vector<double> Price(N+1);
   for (int i=0; i<=N; i++)
   {
      Price[i]=Payoff(Model.S(N,i));
   }
   for (int n=N-1; n>=0; n--)
   {
      for (int i=0; i<=n; i++)
      {
         Price[i]=(q*Price[i+1]+(1-q)*Price[i])
            /(1+Model.GetR());
      }
   }
   return Price[0];
}

double AmOption::PriceBySnell(BinModel Model)
{
   double q=Model.RiskNeutProb();
   int N=GetN();
   vector<double> Price(N+1);
   double ContVal;
   for (int i=0; i<=N; i++)
   {
      Price[i]=Payoff(Model.S(N,i));
   }
   for (int n=N-1; n>=0; n--)
   {
      for (int i=0; i<=n; i++)
      {
         ContVal=(q*Price[i+1]+(1-q)*Price[i])
                        /(1+Model.GetR());
         Price[i]=Payoff(Model.S(n,i));
         if (ContVal>Price[i]) Price[i]=ContVal;
      }
   }
   return Price[0];
}

int Call::GetInputData()
{
   cout << "Enter call option data:" << endl;
   int N;
```

```
   cout << "Enter steps to expiry N: "; cin >> N;
   SetN(N);
   cout << "Enter strike price K:    "; cin >> K;
   cout << endl;
   return 0;
}

double Call::Payoff(double z)
{
   if (z>K) return z-K;
   return 0.0;
}

int Put::GetInputData()
{
   cout << "Enter put option data:" << endl;
   int N;
   cout << "Enter steps to expiry N: "; cin >> N;
   SetN(N);
   cout << "Enter strike price K:    "; cin >> K;
   cout << endl;
   return 0;
}

double Put::Payoff(double z)
{
   if (z<K) return K-z;
   return 0.0;
}
```

Let us analyse the changes.

❶ A new class called Option is introduced. The variable N, function SetN() and virtual function Payoff() are moved into this class.

❷ The line setting N inside GetInputData() has become
   SetN(N);
   No longer will there be a need to set N separately for the EurOption and AmOption classes.

❸ EurOption is declared a subclass of the Option class by
   class EurOption: public virtual Option
   There is a similar line for the AmOption class. These classes no longer explicitly contain N, SetN() or Payoff(), but inherit these members from the Option class.

   There is a new feature here that must be explained: the role of the keyword virtual in this context. This brings us to the topic of **virtual inheritance**.

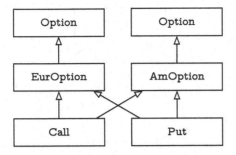

Figure 3.2 Multiple inheritance in Listing 3.4 (virtual inheritance disabled).

Let us temporarily remove the keyword `virtual`, so the above line becomes

```
class EurOption: public Option
```

with a similar change in the corresponding line for the `AmOption` class. When `Optopn02.cpp` is now compiled, an error message will be produced. Depending on the compiler, it may read something like this: 'reference to "Set(N)" is ambiguous'.

The reason for the error message is this. Without virtual inheritance (with the keyword `virtual` removed) the `EurOption` and `AmOption` classes inherit their own distinct copies of N from the `Option` class. In turn, the `Call` class inherits two distinct copies of N, one via the `EurOption` class and one via the `AmOption` class. When the function `Call::GetInputData()` tries to execute `SetN(N)`, it does not know which of these two copies of N is referred to. Similar comments apply to the `Put` class.

This situation is illustrated in Figure 3.2. The `Option` class appears twice in this diagram to indicate that two distinct copies of its members are created in the subclasses.

When virtual inheritance applies (that is, the keyword `virtual` is reinstated), the code compiles and runs without a complaint. In this case a single copy of N (and indeed of any other member of the `Option` class) is shared between the subclasses `EurOption` and `AmOption`. It is this single shared copy of N that is then inherited by the `Call` class as well as by the `Put` class.

Virtual inheritance is illustrated in Figure 3.3. The `Option` class appears once in this diagram, indicating that a single copy of each of its members is shared by the subclasses.

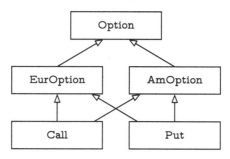

Figure 3.3 Multiple inheritance in Listing 3.4 (virtual inheritance enabled).

④ A new function `int GetN()` is included in the `Option` class. Since `N` is a private member of the `Option` class, this public function is needed to access `N` from the subclasses.

⑤ The `int GetN()` function is used in the line
```
int N=GetN();
```
added to the `PriceByCRR()` and `PriceBySnell()` functions.

There is no change to `Main12.cpp`, except for replacing the line
```
#include "Options07.h"
```
by
```
#include "Options08.h"
```
and renaming the file as `Main13.cpp`, so we do not need to list it here.

3.3 Class templates

We would like to compute and store the price of an American option not only at time 0, but also for each time step n and node i in the binoial tree. In addition, we want to compute the **early exercise policy** for an American option. The time steps n and nodes i at which the option should be exercised are characterised by the condition

$$H(n, i) = h(S(n, i)) > 0.$$

We are going to encode this information as data of type `bool`, taking just two possible values, 0 if the option should not be exercised at a given node, or 1 otherwise, depending on whether the above condition is violated or not.

The natural structure for the price data is that of a lattice indexed by the time steps $n = 0, 1, \ldots, N$ and nodes $i = 0, 1, \ldots, n$ as in diagram (1.1). A convenient way to store the option prices will be a vector indexed by the time variable n consisting vectors of type double indexed by the nodes i at each time n. We wrap this vector of vectors in a class called BinLattice, and provide related functionality such as setting the number of time steps N or setting and retrieving a value at time n and node i.

Listing 3.6   BinLattice01.h

```cpp
#ifndef BinLattice01_h
#define BinLattice01_h

#include <iostream>
#include <iomanip>
#include <vector>
using namespace std;

class BinLattice                                                    ❶
{
   private:
      int N;                                                        ❷
      vector< vector<double> > Lattice;                             ❸

   public:
      void SetN(int N_)                                             ❹
      {
         N=N_;
         Lattice.resize(N+1);
         for(int n=0; n<=N; n++) Lattice[n].resize(n+1);
      }
      void SetNode(int n, int i, double x)                          ❺
         {Lattice[n][i]=x;}
      double GetNode(int n, int i)                                  ❻
         {return Lattice[n][i];}
      void Display()                                                ❼
      {
         cout << setiosflags(ios::fixed)
              << setprecision(3);
         for(int n=0; n<=N; n++)
         {
            for(int i=0; i<=n; i++)
               cout << setw(7) << GetNode(n,i);
            cout << endl;
         }
         cout << endl;
      }
};

#endif
```

❶ The `BinLattice` class is defined here.

The class contains two variables:

❷ `N` to store the number of time steps in the binomial tree,

❸ `Lattice`, a vector of vectors to hold data of type `double`.

The `BinLattice` class also contains the following functions:

❹ The `SetN()` function takes a parameter of type `int`, assigns it to `N`, sets the size of the `Lattice` vector to `N+1`, the number of time instants n from 0 to `N`, and then for each n sets the size of the inner vector `Lattice[n]` to n+1, the number of nodes at time n.

❺ `SetNode()` to set the value stored at step n, node i,

❻ `GetNode()` to return the value stored at step n, node i,

❼ `Display()` to print the values stored in the binomial tree lattice.
   In this function some output formatting features such as fixed decimal point notation are used with `cout`. Refer to a C++ manual to find out more about output formatting.

The entire code for the `BinLattice` class can be found in the header file `BinLattice01.h`, and there is no corresponding `.cpp` file. This breaks with our custom of placing the definitions of more complicated functions such as `Display()` in a `.cpp` file to facilitate separate compilation. The reason is that the `BinLattice` class is going to be converted into a class template, which does not lend itself to separate compilation.

To record the stopping policy, it would be easy enough to write a separate class for data of type `bool` by following the pattern of the `BinLattice` class. However, we do not want the headache of several duplicate code fragments to maintain. Class templates offer a much neater solution. The type is not hardwired inside the class, but passed to it as a parameter. We achieve this by modifying the `BinLattice` class as follows.

Listing 3.7   BinLattice02.h

```
#ifndef BinLattice02_h
#define BinLattice02_h

#include <iostream>
#include <iomanip>
#include <vector>
using namespace std;
```

```
template<typename Type> class BinLattice                         ❶
{
    private:
        int N;
        vector< vector<Type> > Lattice;                          ❷

    public:
        void SetN(int N_)
        {
            N=N_;
            Lattice.resize(N+1);
            for(int n=0; n<=N; n++) Lattice[n].resize(n+1);
        }
        void SetNode(int n, int i, Type x)                       ❸
            {Lattice[n][i]=x;}
        Type GetNode(int n, int i)                               ❹
            {return Lattice[n][i];}
        void Display()
        {
            cout << setiosflags(ios::fixed)
                 << setprecision(3);
            for(int n=0; n<=N; n++)
            {
                for(int i=0; i<=n; i++)
                    cout << setw(7) << GetNode(n,i);
                cout << endl;
            }
            cout << endl;
        }
};

#endif
```

Compared with Listing 3.6, the following changes have been made:

❶ `class BinLattice`
is replaced by
`template<typename Type> class BinLattice`
which specifies that `BinLattice` is no longer a class, but a **class template** with **type parameter** `Type`. Note that the keyword `class` can be used instead of `typename`. (Try it!)

Every occurrence of `double` is replaced by `Type`. In particular:

❷ `vector< vector<double> > Lattice;`
is replaced by
`vector< vector<Type> > Lattice;`

❸ ```
void SetNode(int n, int i, double x)
    {Lattice[n][i]=x;}
```
is replaced by
```
void SetNode(int n, int i, Type x)
    {Lattice[n][i]=x;}
```
❹ ```
double GetNode(int n, int i)
    {return Lattice[n][i];}
```
is replaced by
```
Type GetNode(int n, int i)
    {return Lattice[n][i];}
```

There is no `.cpp` file corresponding to `BinLattice02.h`. A class template can only be compiled after an object has been declared using the template with a specific data type, for example `double`, substituted for the type parameter, and we have not done so yet. Separate compilation will not work for them.

We are ready to modify the `PriceBySnell()` function to compute the option price and exercise policy for each node and store them using the `BinLattice<>` class template.

Listing 3.8   Options09.h

```cpp
#ifndef Options09_h
#define Options09_h

#include "BinLattice02.h"
#include "BinModel02.h"

class Option
{
    private:
        int N; //steps to expiry

    public:
        void SetN(int N_){N=N_;}
        int GetN(){return N;}
        virtual double Payoff(double z)=0;
};

class EurOption: public virtual Option
{
    public:
        //pricing European option
        double PriceByCRR(BinModel Model);
```

```cpp
};

class AmOption: public virtual Option
{
   public:
      //pricing American option
      double PriceBySnell(BinModel Model,
         BinLattice<double>& PriceTree,
         BinLattice<bool>& StoppingTree);
};

class Call: public EurOption, public AmOption
{
   private:
      double K; //strike price

   public:
      void SetK(double K_){K=K_;}
      int GetInputData();
      double Payoff(double z);
};

class Put: public EurOption, public AmOption
{
   private:
      double K; //strike price

   public:
      void SetK(double K_){K=K_;}
      int GetInputData();
      double Payoff(double z);
};

#endif
```

Listing 3.9 Options09.cpp

```cpp
#include "Options09.h"
#include "BinModel02.h"
#include "BinLattice02.h"
#include <iostream>
#include <cmath>
using namespace std;

double EurOption::PriceByCRR(BinModel Model)
{
   double q=Model.RiskNeutProb();
```

```
   int N=GetN();
   vector<double> Price(N+1);
   for (int i=0; i<=N; i++)
   {
      Price[i]=Payoff(Model.S(N,i));
   }
   for (int n=N-1; n>=0; n--)
   {
      for (int i=0; i<=n; i++)
      {
         Price[i]=(q*Price[i+1]+(1-q)*Price[i])
            /(1+Model.GetR());
      }
   }
   return Price[0];
}

double AmOption::PriceBySnell(BinModel Model,
   BinLattice<double>& PriceTree,                          ❶
   BinLattice<bool>& StoppingTree)
{
   double q=Model.RiskNeutProb();
   int N=GetN();
   PriceTree.SetN(N);                                      ❷
   StoppingTree.SetN(N);
   double ContVal;
   for (int i=0; i<=N; i++)
   {
      PriceTree.SetNode(N,i,Payoff(Model.S(N,i)));         ❸
      StoppingTree.SetNode(N,i,1);                         ❹
   }
   for (int n=N-1; n>=0; n--)
   {
      for (int i=0; i<=n; i++)
      {
         ContVal=(q*PriceTree.GetNode(n+1,i+1)
            +(1-q)*PriceTree.GetNode(n+1,i))
            /(1+Model.GetR());
         PriceTree.SetNode(n,i,Payoff(Model.S(n,i)));
         StoppingTree.SetNode(n,i,1);                      ❹
         if (ContVal>PriceTree.GetNode(n,i))
         {
            PriceTree.SetNode(n,i,ContVal);
            StoppingTree.SetNode(n,i,0);                   ❹
         }
         else if (PriceTree.GetNode(n,i)==0.0)
         {
            StoppingTree.SetNode(n,i,0);                   ❹
         }
```

```
        }
    }
    return PriceTree.GetNode(0,0);
}

int Call::GetInputData()
{
    cout << "Enter call option data:" << endl;
    int N;
    cout << "Enter steps to expiry N: "; cin >> N;
    SetN(N);
    cout << "Enter strike price K:    "; cin >> K;
    cout << endl;
    return 0;
}

double Call::Payoff(double z)
{
    if (z>K) return z-K;
    return 0.0;
}

int Put::GetInputData()
{
    cout << "Enter put option data:" << endl;
    int N;
    cout << "Enter steps to expiry N: "; cin >> N;
    SetN(N);
    cout << "Enter strike price K:    "; cin >> K;
    cout << endl;
    return 0;
}

double Put::Payoff(double z)
{
    if (z<K) return K-z;
    return 0.0;
}
```

The following changes have been made in the `PriceBySnell()` function from Listings 3.4 and 3.5:

❶ Two new objects `PriceTree` and `StoppingTree` are passed by reference to `PriceBySnell()`. We want the values computed and placed at the nodes to remain available after the function terminates.

Here `PriceTree` is an object of `BinLattice<double>` class, to all ends and purposes equivalent to the `BinLattice` class from Listing 3.6. Similarly, `StoppingTree` is an object of `BinLattice<bool>` class.

The compiler can generate different classes from the `BinLattice<>` template. This is achieved by substituting specific type names for the type parameter within the angular brackets `<>`.

❷ The size of the `PriceTree` and `StoppingTree` is determined by the number of steps to expiry for the option.

❸ The `Price` vector has become redundant in `PriceBySnell()`, its role taken over by `PriceTree`.

❹ New lines of code are added within the body of `PriceBySnell()` to set the appropriate values of `bool` type in the `StoppingTree` lattice.

Finally, in `main()` we compute and display the price tree and stopping policy tree for an American put.

Listing 3.10   Main14.cpp

```
#include "BinLattice02.h"
#include "BinModel02.h"
#include "Options09.h"
#include <iostream>
using namespace std;

int main()
{
   BinModel Model;

   if (Model.GetInputData()==1) return 1;

   Put Option;
   Option.GetInputData();
   BinLattice<double> PriceTree;                                    ❶
   BinLattice<bool> StoppingTree;
   Option.PriceBySnell(Model,PriceTree,StoppingTree);               ❷
   cout << "American put prices:" << endl << endl;
   PriceTree.Display();                                             ❸
   cout << "American put exercise policy:"
        << endl << endl;
   StoppingTree.Display();                                          ❸
   return 0;
}
```

❶ `BinLattice<double> PriceTree;`
  `BinLattice<bool> StoppingTree;`
  create objects `PriceTree` and `StoppingTree`.

❷ `Option.PriceBySnell(Model,PriceTree,StoppingTree);`
  is called to compute the option prices and stopping policy for all nodes
  and store them inside `PriceTree` and `StoppingTree`.

❸ `PriceTree.Display();`
  displays the prices for all nodes, and
  `StoppingTree.Display();`
  displays the stopping policy, that is, 1s for the nodes where the American option should be exercised (unless exercised already), and 0s for
  the others.

Exercise 3.1 Modify the `PriceByCRR()` function in `Options09.h`
and `Options09.cpp` to compute the replicating strategy for a European option in the binomial tree model, using the `BinLattice<>`
class template to store the stock and money market account positions
in the replicating strategy at the nodes of the binomial tree.

The portfolio belonging to the **replicating strategy** created at time
$n - 1$, node i and held during the nth time step, that is, until time n,
consists of stock and money market account positions

$$x(n, i) = \frac{H(n, i + 1) - H(n, i)}{S(n, i + 1) - S(n, i)}, \tag{3.3}$$

$$y(n, i) = \frac{H(n - 1, i) - x(n, i)S(n - 1, i)}{(1 + R)^{n-1}}, \tag{3.4}$$

for $n = 1, 2, \ldots, N$ and $i = 0, 1, \ldots, n - 1$, where $S(n, i)$ and $H(n, i)$
denote the stock and option prices at time n, node i. (For details, see
[DMFM].)

Exercise 3.2 The binomial model can be employed to approximate
the Black–Scholes model. One of several possible approximation
schemes is the following. Divide the time interval $[0, T]$ into N steps
of length $h = \frac{T}{N}$, and set the parameters of the binomial model to be

$$U = e^{(r+\sigma^2/2)h+\sigma\sqrt{h}} - 1,$$
$$D = e^{(r+\sigma^2/2)h-\sigma\sqrt{h}} - 1,$$
$$R = e^{rh} - 1,$$

where σ is the volatility and r is the continuously compounded interest rate in the Black–Scholes model.

Develop code to compute the approximate price for an American put option in the Black–Scholes model by means of this binomial tree approximation.

In addition to class templates, C++ also allows function templates. Their setup is similar to class templates as illustrated by Exercise 3.3 below. In Section 4.6 function templates will be put to work as an alternative to virtual functions to improve the efficiency of numerical computations.

Exercise 3.3   The function in Exercise 1.2 interchanges the contents of two variables of type `double`. Read about function templates from a C++ manual, and turn this function into a function template designed to interchange the contents of two variables of any given type. Test this function template, using it to interchange the contents of variables of various types.

4

Non-linear solvers

In finance we frequently encounter the need to compute numerical solutions to non-linear equations. Typical examples include computing implied volatility (see Sections 4.1 and 4.7) and computing the yield of a fixed coupon bond (Exercise 4.2).

There are several well-known numerical methods for solving non-linear equations. The simplest of these are the bisection method and the Newton–Raphson method. We are going to develop three implementations of these methods: by means of function pointers, virtual functions and function templates, comparing their advantages and disadvantages.

Two of these programming approaches, namely function pointers and virtual functions, we have used before, and this is an opportunity to rehearse them more thoroughly. Using function templates in place of function pointers or virtual functions is a new technique, elegant and computationally efficient, which we are going to learn in this chapter.

4.1 Implied volatility

Within the Black–Scholes model the price of a European call option with expiry time T and strike price K is given by the **Black–Scholes formula**

$$C(S(0), K, T, \sigma, r) = S(0)N(d_+) - Ke^{-rT}N(d_-) \qquad (4.1)$$

75

with

$$d_+ = \frac{\ln(S(0)/K) + (r + \sigma^2/2)T}{\sigma\sqrt{T}}, \quad d_- = d_+ - \sigma\sqrt{T}, \qquad (4.2)$$

where $S(0)$ is the price of the underlying stock (the spot price), σ is the stock volatility, r is the continuously compounded interest rate, and where

$$N(x) = \int_{-\infty}^{x} \frac{1}{\sqrt{2\pi}} e^{-y^2/2} dy \qquad (4.3)$$

is the distribution function of the standard normal distribution $N(0, 1)$ with mean 0 and variance 1. For details, see [BSM].

If the values of $S(0), K, T, \sigma, r$ are all known, then (4.1) can be used to compute the option price predicted by the Black–Scholes model. Among these variables, T and K are known quantities written into the option contract. Quotes for the current stock price $S(0)$ and interest rate r are also readily available. However, the volatility σ is not, and needs to be estimated from market data.

One popular way of estimating σ is to look up the market price C_{quote} quoted for some European call option and then to solve the non-linear equation

$$C(S(0), K, T, \sigma, r) = C_{\text{quote}} \qquad (4.4)$$

for σ, given the known values of $S(0), K, T, r$. The solution σ, called **implied volatility**, can then be used to price and hedge options of other kinds.

4.2 Bisection method

We want to compute a solution x to an equation

$$f(x) = c,$$

where f is a given function from an interval $[a, b]$ to $\mathbb{R}$. It is assumed that f is continuous on $[a, b]$ and $f(a) - c, f(b) - c$ have opposite signs. Then there must be an $x \in [a, b]$ such that $f(x) = c$.

The bisection method works by constructing sequences l_n, r_n of left and right approximations by induction:

- Let

$$l_0 = a, \quad r_0 = b.$$

- If l_n and r_n have already been constructed for some $n = 0, 1, 2, \ldots$, let

$$l_{n+1} = l_n, \quad r_{n+1} = \tfrac{1}{2}(l_n + r_n)$$

if $f(l_n) - c$ and $f(\frac{1}{2}(l_n + r_n)) - c$ have opposite signs, and

$$l_{n+1} = \tfrac{1}{2}(l_n + r_n), \quad r_{n+1} = r_n$$

otherwise.

Then $l_n \nearrow x$ and $r_n \searrow x$ as $n \to \infty$, where $x \in [a, b]$ is a solution to $f(x) = c$.

4.3 Newton–Raphson method

In this case f is assumed to be differentiable on $[a, b]$. We construct a sequence x_n as follows:

- Take

$$x_0 \in (a, b).$$

- For $n = 0, 1, 2, \ldots$ let

$$x_{n+1} = x_n - \frac{f(x_n) - c}{f'(x_n)}.$$

If the equation $f(x) = c$ has a solution $x \in (a, b)$ such that $f'(x) \neq 0$ and x_0 is chosen close enough to x, then x_n will converge to x.

4.4 Function pointers

Implementation using function pointers is straightforward.

Listing 4.1 **Solver01.h**

```
#ifndef Solver01_h
#define Solver01_h

double SolveByBisect(double(*Fct)(double x),          ❶
    double Tgt, double LEnd, double REnd, double Acc)
{
    double left=LEnd, right=REnd, mid=(left+right)/2;
    double y_left=Fct(left)-Tgt, y_mid=Fct(mid)-Tgt;
    while (mid-left>Acc)
    {
        if ((y_left>0 && y_mid>0)||(y_left<0 && y_mid<0))
            {left=mid; y_left=y_mid;}
        else right=mid;
```

```
          mid=(left+right)/2;
          y_mid=Fct(mid)-Tgt;
      }
      return mid;
}

double SolveByNR(double(*Fct)(double x),                    ❷
      double(*DFct)(double x),
      double Tgt, double Guess, double Acc)
{
      double x_prev=Guess;
      double x_next=x_prev-(Fct(x_prev)-Tgt)/DFct(x_prev);
      while (x_next-x_prev>Acc || x_prev-x_next>Acc)
      {
         x_prev=x_next;
         x_next=x_prev-(Fct(x_prev)-Tgt)/DFct(x_prev);
      }
      return x_next;
}

#endif
```

❶ The function `SolveByBisect()` is defined to implement the bisection method.

It takes a function pointer `Fct` as an argument, so a function f can be passed to the solver. In addition, `SolveByBisect()` takes arguments `Tgt` for the target value c of the function, `LEnd` and `REnd` for the left and right endpoints of the interval $[a, b]$, and `Acc` for the desired accuracy of the numerical solution, which will determine when the algorithm should be stopped.

Care is taken in `SolveByBisect()` that only one evaluation of f is made for each loop iteration in order to speed up computation. This results in slightly more complicated code than may seem necessary, namely the introduction of the variables `y_left` and `y_mid` to carry values of the function between loop iterations. The price is worth paying because the bisection method is not lightning fast.

Checking whether or not $f(a) - c, f(b) - c$ have opposite signs to begin with is omitted in `SolveByBisect()` for simplicity.

❷ `SolveByNR()` implements the Newton–Raphson solver.

It takes two function pointers `Fct` and `DFct` so that both a function f and its derivative f' can be passed. Moreover, `SolveByNR()` also takes arguments `Tgt` for the target value c, `Guess` for the initial term x_0 of the approximating sequence, and `Acc` for the desired accuracy to be reached before the algorithm is terminated.

The iterations x_n will converge to an x such that $f(x) = c$ if $f'(x) \neq 0$ and x_0 is close enough to x. In this case the algorithm will be terminated after the prescribed accuracy is reached. In other circumstances `SolveByNR()` may enter an infinite loop. This ought to be prevented, for example by setting an upper limit on the number of iterations, but it is not, for simplicity.

The following code shows how to solve the equation $f(x) = 0$ for $f(x) = x^2 - 2$ by means of `SolveByBisect()` and `SolveByNR()`.

Listing 4.2 Main15.cpp

```cpp
#include "Solver01.h"
#include <iostream>
using namespace std;

double F1(double x){return x*x-2;}
double DF1(double x){return 2*x;}

int main()
{
    double Acc=0.001;
    double LEnd=0.0, REnd=2.0;
    double Tgt=0.0;
    cout << "Root of F1 by bisect: "
         << SolveByBisect(F1,Tgt,LEnd,REnd,Acc)
         << endl;
    double Guess=1.0;
    cout << "Root of F1 by Newton-Raphson: "
         << SolveByNR(F1,DF1,Tgt,Guess,Acc)
         << endl;
    return 0;
}
```

Function pointers are simple enough, but limit the possibilities for expansion. The code can readily be adapted for other functions $f(x)$ with a single argument x, but it would not be easy to handle a function with a parameter, for example $f(x, a) = x^2 - a$. The type of the function pointer is hardwired as `double(*Fct)(double x)`, which does not allow for extra parameters.

When solving (4.4) for implied volatility σ, we have the option price $C(T, K, S, \sigma, r)$ given as a function of σ and several other parameters. We have already encountered a similar problem in Section 1.8 when trying to include option payoffs with more parameters than just the strike price, and learnt in Section 2.4 that virtual functions can help.

4.5 Virtual functions

We recycle as much as possible of the code from the last section, replacing function pointers by classes and virtual functions.

Listing 4.3   Solver02.h

```
#ifndef Solver02_h
#define Solver02_h

class Function                                                    ❶
{
    public:
        virtual double Value(double x)=0;
        virtual double Deriv(double x)=0;
};

double SolveByBisect(Function* Fct,                               ❷
    double Tgt, double LEnd, double REnd, double Acc)
{
    double left=LEnd, right=REnd, mid=(left+right)/2;
    double y_left=Fct->Value(left)-Tgt, y_mid=Fct->Value(mid)-Tgt;
    while (mid-left>Acc)
    {
        if ((y_left>0 && y_mid>0)||(y_left<0 && y_mid<0))
            {left=mid; y_left=y_mid;}
        else right=mid;
        mid=(left+right)/2;
        y_mid=Fct->Value(mid)-Tgt;
    }
    return mid;
}

double SolveByNR(Function* Fct,                                   ❷
    double Tgt, double Guess, double Acc)
{
    double x_prev=Guess;
    double x_next=x_prev
        -(Fct->Value(x_prev)-Tgt)/Fct->Deriv(x_prev);
    while (x_next-x_prev>Acc || x_prev-x_next>Acc)
    {
        x_prev=x_next;
```

```
        x_next=x_prev
            -(Fct->Value(x_prev)-Tgt)/Fct->Deriv(x_prev);
    }
    return x_next;
}

#endif
```

❶ An abstract class called `Function` is introduced to represent a general function f. The class has two pure virtual member functions: `Value()` to return the value of f at x, and `Deriv()` to return the value of the derivative f' at x.

❷ `Fct` is passed to `SolveByBisect()` and `SolveByNR()` no longer as a function pointer but as a pointer to the `Function` class. We need to work with a pointer to this class to take advantage of virtual functions.

`DFct`, the function pointer passed to `SolveByNR()` in the previous version to compute the derivative is no longer needed. `Deriv()` is now a member of the `Function` class, and both `Value()` and `Deriv()` can be accessed through the pointer `Fct` to this class.

For example, `Fct->Value(x_prev)` returns the value of the function at `x_prev`, and `Fct->Deriv(x_prev)` returns the derivative at `x_prev`.

Note the operator `->`. It should be used when a function that is a member of a class is called with a pointer to an object of that class (or a subclass).

Some concrete functions can now be introduced as subclasses of the `Function` class, and then the solvers called to do their business.

Listing 4.4   Main16.cpp

```
#include "Solver02.h"
#include <iostream>
using namespace std;

class F1: public Function                              ❶
{
    public:
        double Value(double x){return x*x-2;}          ❷
        double Deriv(double x){return 2*x;}
} MyF1;                                                 ❸
```

```
class F2: public Function                                    ❹
{
   private:
      double a; //parameter
   public:
      F2(double a_){a=a_;}                                    ❺
      double Value(double x){return x*x-a;}
      double Deriv(double x){return 2*x;}
} MyF2(3.0);                                                  ❻

int main()
{
   double Acc=0.001;
   double LEnd=0.0, REnd=2.0;
   double Tgt=0.0;
   cout << "Root of F1 by bisect: "
        << SolveByBisect(&MyF1,Tgt,LEnd,REnd,Acc)             ❼
        << endl;
   cout << "Root of F2 by bisect: "
        << SolveByBisect(&MyF2,Tgt,LEnd,REnd,Acc)             ❼
        << endl;
   double Guess=1.0;
   cout << "Root of F1 by Newton-Raphson: "
        << SolveByNR(&MyF1,Tgt,Guess,Acc)                     ❼
        << endl;
   cout << "Root of F2 by Newton-Raphson: "
        << SolveByNR(&MyF2,Tgt,Guess,Acc)                     ❼
        << endl;
   return 0;
}
```

❶ Class `F1`, a subclass of the `Function` class, corresponds to the old function `F1()` in the previous version.

❷ The `Value()` function belonging to the class `F1` is in fact the old function `F1()`, whereas `Deriv()` is the old `DF1()`.

❸ Note that an object `MyF1` of class `F1` is created as part of the definition of the class. This is just to illustrate this possibility. Alternatively, we could remove `MyF1` preceding the closing semicolon at the end of the definition of class `F1`, and include a separate line
`F1 MyF1;`
The effect would be the same.

❹ Class `F2` is also a subclass of the `Function` class. This one, however, defines a function with a parameter, namely $f(x, a) = x^2 - a$, something that was hard to do with function pointers.

❺ Class F2 contains a constructor function
`F2(double a_){a=a_;}`
so that the value of a can be set when creating an object of class F2.

❻ An object MyF2 of class F2 is created as part of the definition of the class, with a initiated with the value 3.0.

❼ Another noteworthy feature is that the pointers &MyF1 and &MyF2 rather than MyF1 and MyF2 themselves are passed to SolveByBisect() and SolveByNR(). This is needed for the virtual functions to work inside the solvers. They expect a pointer to an object of the parent class here, but instead receive the pointer &MyF1 or &MyF2 to an object belonging to a subclass. When the virtual functions Value() or Deriv() are called with this pointer, they do their checking at run time and select the correct version to be executed.

4.6 Function templates

The code with virtual functions is elegant and works as expected. However, there is a price to pay to have type checking performed at run time. Because it occurs inside a loop, it will happen repeatedly, possibly creating noticeable computing time overheads.

It is not a significant issue here because the loops go through a few iterations only for the prescribed accuracy. (Try to figure out how many!) But it is not hard to imagine a situation, perhaps involving multiple nested loops with millions of iterations, when it would pay to work harder to improve efficiency.

Templates offer a technique that largely retains the advantages of virtual functions over function pointers, but shifts type checking from run time to compile time. In some cases of heavy numerical computations this could mean measurable runtime savings for the end user.

There is never a free lunch, and templates come with their own set of problems. These will be pointed out later, once we have examined the code.

Listing 4.5 Solver03.h

```
#ifndef Solver03_h
#define Solver03_h

template<typename Function> double SolveByBisect        ❶
```

```
   (Function* Fct,
   double Tgt, double LEnd, double REnd, double Acc)
{
   double left=LEnd, right=REnd, mid=(left+right)/2;
   double y_left=Fct->Value(left)-Tgt, y_mid=Fct->Value(mid)-Tgt;
   while (mid-left>Acc)
   {
      if ((y_left>0 && y_mid>0)||(y_left<0 && y_mid<0))
         {left=mid; y_left=y_mid;}
      else right=mid;
      mid=(left+right)/2;
      y_mid=Fct->Value(mid)-Tgt;
   }
   return mid;
}

template<typename Function> double SolveByNR
   (Function* Fct,
   double Tgt, double Guess, double Acc)
{
   double x_prev=Guess;
   double x_next=x_prev
      -(Fct->Value(x_prev)-Tgt)/Fct->Deriv(x_prev);
   while (x_next-x_prev>Acc || x_prev-x_next>Acc)
   {
      x_prev=x_next;
      x_next=x_prev
         -(Fct->Value(x_prev)-Tgt)/Fct->Deriv(x_prev);
   }
   return x_next;
}

#endif
```

❶

Listing 4.6   Main17.cpp

```
#include "Solver03.h"
#include <iostream>
using namespace std;

class F1
{
   public:
      double Value(double x){return x*x-2;}
      double Deriv(double x){return 2*x;}
} MyF1;
```

❷

```
class F2                                                          ❷
{
    private:
        double a; //parameter
    public:
        F2(double a_){a=a_;}
        double Value(double x){return x*x-a;}
        double Deriv(double x){return 2*x;}
} MyF2(3.0);

int main()
{
    double Acc=0.001;
    double LEnd=0.0, REnd=2.0;
    double Tgt=0.0;
    cout << "Root of F1 by bisect: "
         << SolveByBisect(&MyF1,Tgt,LEnd,REnd,Acc)
         << endl;
    cout << "Root of F2 by bisect: "
         << SolveByBisect(&MyF2,Tgt,LEnd,REnd,Acc)
         << endl;
    double Guess=1.0;
    cout << "Root of F1 by Newton-Raphson: "
         << SolveByNR(&MyF1,Tgt,Guess,Acc)
         << endl;
    cout << "Root of F2 by Newton-Raphson: "
         << SolveByNR(&MyF2,Tgt,Guess,Acc)
         << endl;
    return 0;
}
```

Some interesting things happen in this version.

❶ Function has become a template parameter. The Function class is gone. Gone with it are the pure virtual functions.

The old functions SolveByBisect() and SolveByNR() have become **function templates**.

❷ F1 and F2 are no longer subclasses of anything because the parent class is gone.

It is remarkable how few changes are necessary to templatise the code. Arguably, things have been simplified given that the abstract class and virtual functions have disappeared, and no inheritance is involved.

The compiler can decide how to compile the template functions by looking at the first parameter passed to `SolveByBisect()` and `SolveByNR()`. If `&MyF1` is passed, it substitutes class `F1` for the parameter `Function` when compiling the code. When `&MyF2` is passed, then it substitutes `F2`, and compiles another version of the code. There will be two different versions of `SolveByBisect()`, one to work with class `F1` and one with class `F2`, as well as two versions of `SolveByNR()` in the compiled code.

If more functions were involved, each with its own class, there would be even more versions of `SolveByBisect()` and `SolveByNR()` in the compiled code. This can result in long compile times and large `.exe` files. It may or may not be a price worth paying for gains in the speed of computation at run time.

Because we no longer work with virtual functions, using pointers is unnecessary. The code could be simplified further by changing the type of the argument `Fct` passed to `SolveByBisect()` and `SolveByNR()` from a pointer to `Function` to an object of type `Function`. This will be done in Exercise 4.1.

Exercise 4.1 Alter the code in `Solver03.h` and `Main17.cpp` to have an object of type `Function` passed by reference to `SolveByBisect()` and `SolveByNR()` rather than having a pointer to an object of type `Function` passed to them.

Exercise 4.2 The **yield** y of a coupon bond with face value F, maturity T, and fixed coupons $C_1, \ldots, C_N$ payable at times $0 < T_1 < \cdots < T_n = T$ satisfies

$$P = \sum_{n=1}^{N} C_n e^{-yT_n} + F e^{-yT}, \qquad (4.5)$$

where P is the bond price at time 0.

Using `Solver03.h`, write a program to compute the yield y of a coupon bond by solving the non-linear equation (4.5).

Exercise 4.3 Rewrite the code for numerical integration in Exercises 2.1 and 2.3 replacing function pointers/virtual functions by templates.

> **Exercise 4.4**   Rewrite the code for option pricing in `Options09.h`, `Options09.cpp` and `Main14.cpp`, replacing virtual functions by templates.

4.7 Computing implied volatility

We are going to use the solvers developed in the preceding section to compute implied volatility.

First of all, we implement a class representing a European call option in the Black–Scholes model, complete with a function for computing the option price by means of the Black–Scholes formula (4.1).

This requires, in particular, computing the distribution function $N(x)$ for the normal distribution $N(0, 1)$. The distribution function is given by (4.3), but it can be implemented more efficiently using the following rational function approximation:

$$N(x) \approx \begin{cases} 1 - \frac{1}{\sqrt{2\pi}} e^{-\frac{1}{2}x^2} \left(a_1 k + a_2 k^2 + a_3 k^3 + a_4 k^4 + a_5 k^5 \right) & \text{if } x \geq 0, \\ 1 - N(-x) & \text{if } x < 0, \end{cases}$$

(4.6)

where $k = (1 + \gamma x)^{-1}$, and where $\gamma, a_1, a_2, a_3, a_4, a_5$ are suitably chosen constants (see function `N()` in Listing 4.8 for their values).

To compute the implied volatility using the Newton–Raphson solver, we also need an expression for the derivative of the European call option price with respect to volatility σ. This derivative, called **vega**, is given by

$$v = \frac{1}{\sqrt{2\pi}} S(0) \exp\left(\frac{-d_+^2}{2}\right)$$

(4.7)

in the Black–Scholes model, where d_+ is expressed by (4.2).

Listing 4.7   EurCall.h

```
#ifndef EurCall_h
#define EurCall_h

class EurCall                                    ❶
{
    public:
```

```
        double T, K;
        EurCall(double T_, double K_){T=T_; K=K_;}
        double d_plus(double S0, double sigma, double r);      ❸
        double d_minus(double S0, double sigma, double r);
        double PriceByBSFormula(double S0,                     ❹
            double sigma, double r);
        double VegaByBSFormula(double S0,                      ❺
            double sigma, double r);
};

#endif
```

Listing 4.8   EurCall.cpp

```
#include "EurCall.h"
#include <cmath>

double N(double x)                                            ❷
{
   double gamma = 0.2316419;     double a1 = 0.319381530;
   double a2    =-0.356563782;   double a3 = 1.781477937;
   double a4    =-1.821255978;   double a5 = 1.330274429;
   double pi    = 4.0*atan(1.0); double k  = 1.0/(1.0+gamma*x);
   if (x>=0.0)
   {
      return 1.0-(((((a5*k+a4)*k+a3)*k+a2)*k+a1)
              *k*exp(-x*x/2.0)/sqrt(2.0*pi);
   }
   else return 1.0-N(-x);
}

double EurCall::d_plus(double S0, double sigma, double r)     ❸
{
   return (log(S0/K)+
      (r+0.5*pow(sigma,2.0))*T)
      /(sigma*sqrt(T));
}

double EurCall::d_minus(double S0, double sigma, double r)   ❸
{
   return d_plus(S0,sigma,r)-sigma*sqrt(T);
}

double EurCall::PriceByBSFormula(double S0,                  ❹
   double sigma, double r)
```

```
{
   return S0*N(d_plus(S0,sigma,r))
      -K*exp(-r*T)*N(d_minus(S0,sigma,r));
}

double EurCall::VegaByBSFormula(double S0,                    ❺
   double sigma, double r)
{
   double pi=4.0*atan(1.0);
   return S0*exp(-d_plus(S0,sigma,r)*d_plus(S0,sigma,r)/2)*sqrt(T)
      /sqrt(2.0*pi);
}
```

❶ The `EurCall` class contains the variables T, K characterising the call option and a constructor function to initialise these variables. There are also functions for computing the option price and vega, and also auxiliary functions to compute d_+ and d_-. There is no need for this class to contain the payoff function, which is not going to be used explicitly in this context.

❷ The distribution function $N(x)$ is computed using the rational function approximation (4.6). Here we see the values of the constants γ and a_1, a_2, a_3, a_4, a_5 in (4.6).

❸ These functions compute d_+ and d_- from (4.2).

❹ The function `PriceByBSFormula()` computes the option price from the Black–Scholes formula (4.1).

❺ `VegaByBSFormula()` computes the vega parameter from (4.7).

We are going to use the templatised solvers from Listing 4.5 to compute implied volatility. To this end we need to create a class containing functions `Value()` and `Deriv()` connected, respectively, to the functions for the option price and vega in the `EurCall` class. This is done and then used to compute the impled volatility in the next piece of code.

Listing 4.9 Main18.cpp

```
#include "Solver03.h"
#include "EurCall.h"
#include <iostream>
using namespace std;
```

```
class Intermediary: public EurCall                              ❶
{
    private:
        double S0,r;
    public:
        Intermediary(double S0_, double r_, double T_, double K_)
            : EurCall(T_,K_) {S0=S0_; r=r_;}                    ❷
        double Value(double sigma)                              ❸
        {
            return PriceByBSFormula(S0,sigma,r);
        }
        double Deriv(double sigma)                              ❹
        {
            return VegaByBSFormula(S0,sigma,r);
        }
};

int main()
{
    double S0=100.0;
    double r=0.1;
    double T=1.0;
    double K=100.0;
    Intermediary Call(S0,r,T,K);                                ❺

    double Acc=0.001;
    double LEnd=0.01, REnd=1.0;
    double Tgt=12.56;                                           ❻
    cout << "Implied vol by bisect: "
         << SolveByBisect(&Call,Tgt,LEnd,REnd,Acc)              ❼
         << endl;
    double Guess=0.23;
    cout << "Implied vol by Newton-Raphson: "
         << SolveByNR(&Call,Tgt,Guess,Acc)                      ❽
         << endl;
    return 0;
}
```

❶ We need an intermediary between the `EurCall` class and the solvers, translating `PriceByBSFormula()` and `VegaByBSFormula()` into the `Value()` and `Deriv()` functions, which the solvers can understand. The subclass `Intermediary` of the `EurCall` class is in charge of this job.

❷ The constructor function of the `Intermediary` class calls the constructor of the `EurCall` class to initiate `T`, `K`, and then initiates `S0`, `r`.

❸ `Value()` is connected to `PriceByBSFormula()`.

❹ `Deriv()` is connected to `VegaByBSFormula()`.

❺ An object `Call` of the `Intermediary` class is declared and the parameters of this object are initiated.

❻ `Tgt` is initiated with the observed call price C_{quote}.

❼ Implied volatility is computed by the bisection solver.

❽ Implied volatility is computed by the Newton–Raphson solver.

4.8 Remarks on templates

One difficulty with templates is that they are prone to programming bugs and can be harder to debug than code without templates, producing mystifying compiler errors. On the other hand, templates capturing some generic data structures and tasks can save a huge amount of coding, reducing the scope for errors and improving readability.

When using templates, proceed with caution:

- Carefully consider alternative techniques, balancing the pros and cons.
- First write a specific version with no templates and with typical data types in place of template parameters. Test and debug the code thoroughly before templatising it.

  We followed this procedure when developing the templates in Sections 3.3 and 4.6.
- When documenting templates, take care to specify any restrictions on the object types that can be substituted for template parameters.

  For example, only classes that have public member functions `Value()` and `Deriv()` consistent with the prototypes
  ```
  double Value(double x);
  double Deriv(double x);
  ```
  will work when substituted in place of the `Function` parameter in the templates `SolveByBisect()` and `SolveByNR()`.
- Use templates for relatively small generic tasks and structures that are likely to be recycled in several different contexts. Larger or more specific tasks might be better off without templates, except perhaps for running time considerations when relevant.

  For example, a template for a pair or for a sequence of objects is very likely to be re-used many times. A template for a solver is likely to be used with many different function types. An option payoff might also lend itself well to templatising as there are many different types of payoff function, each one relatively simple, and payoffs tend to be evaluated repeatedly inside a loop when pricing options.

On the other hand, a full-scale option pricer would seem an unlikely candidate for templatising, as it would be too large and too specific.

5

Monte Carlo methods

Consider a game of heads and tails. We suspect that the coin is not symmetric, and want to investigate how this influences the game. A simple solution would be to toss the coin many times, and to compute the average of the outcomes. This way we can estimate the expected outcome of the game. Such computation of expectation is the underlying idea behind Monte Carlo methods.

5.1 Path-dependent options

In this chapter we price options under the Black–Scholes model. We consider a money market account

$$A(t) = e^{rt},$$

where $t \geq 0$ is the time and $r \in \mathbb{R}$ is the risk-free rate under continuous compounding. We also consider a risky asset

$$S(t) = S(0)e^{\left(r - \frac{\sigma^2}{2}\right)t + \sigma W_Q(t)}, \tag{5.1}$$

where $\sigma \in \mathbb{R}$ is the volatility and $W_Q(t)$ is a Wiener process under the risk-neutral probability Q. For more details on the Black–Scholes model see [BSM].

Let $t_k = \frac{k}{m}T$ for $k = 1, \ldots, m$. A **path-dependent option** is a financial derivative with payoff at expiry date T

$$H(T) = h(S(t_1), \ldots, S(t_m)), \qquad (5.2)$$

where $h : \mathbb{R}^m \to \mathbb{R}$ is a given deterministic payoff function. A typical example of a path-dependent option is the **arithmetic Asian call**, where the payoff function is given by

$$h^{\text{arithm Asian call}}(z_1, \ldots, z_m) = \left(\frac{1}{m} \sum_{k=1}^{m} z_i - K \right)^+. \qquad (5.3)$$

We denote the price of a path-dependent option by $H(0)$. The price can be determined by computing the expected discounted payoff under Q

$$H(0) = e^{-rT} \mathbb{E}_Q(H(T)). \qquad (5.4)$$

In the majority of cases, including the arithmetic Asian call, such expectation cannot be computed analytically. Below we shall show how the expectation can be computed using Monte Carlo.

The Wiener process W_Q has independent increments, with $W_Q(t) - W_Q(s)$ having normal distribution $N(0, t - s)$ for any $t > s \geq 0$. From (5.1), $S(t_k)$ can therefore be expressed as

$$S(t_k) = S(t_{k-1})e^{\left(r - \frac{\sigma^2}{2}\right)(t_k - t_{k-1}) + \sigma \sqrt{t_k - t_{k-1}} Z_k}, \qquad (5.5)$$

where $Z_1, \ldots, Z_m$ are independent and identically distributed (i.i.d.) random variables with distribution $N(0, 1)$.

Let $\hat{Z}_1, \ldots, \hat{Z}_k$ be a sequence of independent samples of $Z_1, \ldots, Z_k$, respectively. We refer to the sequence

$$\left(\hat{S}(t_1), \ldots, \hat{S}(t_m) \right), \qquad (5.6)$$

defined by

$$\hat{S}(t_1) = S(0)e^{\left(r - \frac{\sigma^2}{2}\right)t_1 + \sigma \sqrt{t_1} \hat{Z}_1}, \qquad (5.7)$$

$$\hat{S}(t_k) = \hat{S}(t_{k-1})e^{\left(r - \frac{\sigma^2}{2}\right)(t_k - t_{k-1}) + \sigma \sqrt{t_k - t_{k-1}} \hat{Z}_k}, \quad \text{for } k = 2, \ldots, m,$$

as a **sample path** (see Figure 5.1).

Let $(\hat{S}^i(t_1), \ldots, \hat{S}^i(t_m))$, for $i \in \mathbb{N}$, be a sequence of independent sample paths. By the law of large numbers

$$\mathbb{E}_Q(h(S(t_1), \ldots, S(t_m))) = \lim_{N \to \infty} \frac{1}{N} \sum_{i=1}^{N} h(\hat{S}^i(t_1), \ldots, \hat{S}^i(t_m)). \qquad (5.8)$$

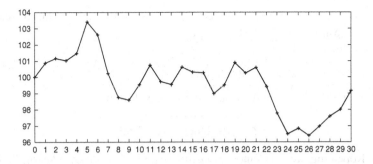

Figure 5.1 A sample path for stock starting at 100, over a 30-day period.

This means that for sufficiently large N, by (5.2), (5.4) and (5.8), we can approximate $H(0)$ using

$$H(0) \approx \hat{H}_N(0) = e^{-rT} \frac{1}{N} \sum_{i=1}^{N} h(\hat{S}^i(t_1), \ldots, \hat{S}^i(t_m)). \qquad (5.9)$$

Sample paths can be generated on a computer. This makes (5.9) a practical tool for the pricing of path-dependent options.

5.2 Valuation

We start by showing how to generate samples of random variables with standard normal distribution.

In C++ we have at our disposal a function `rand()`, which generates integer numbers, simulating a sequence of i.i.d. random variables, uniformly distributed within the range from 0 to `RAND_MAX` . We now give a theorem that will allow us to generate a random number with distribution $N(0, 1)$.

Theorem 5.1 Box–Muller method
If U_1, U_2 are independent random variables with uniform distribution on an interval $[0, 1]$, then the random variable

$$Z = \sqrt{-2\ln(U_1)} \cos(2\pi U_2) \qquad (5.10)$$

has distribution $N(0, 1)$.

For the proof of the theorem see [PF].

We can use Theorem 5.1 to produce the following recipe for generating sample paths:

(i) Generate two integer numbers k_1 and k_2 using `rand()`, and rescale the results to lie in [0, 1], computing

$$\hat{U}_l = \frac{k_l + 1}{\text{RAND\_MAX} + 1} \quad \text{for } l = 1, 2. \tag{5.11}$$

(ii) Using (5.10) compute a sample $\hat{Z}$ of Z as follows:

$$\hat{Z} = \sqrt{-2 \ln(\hat{U}_1)} \cos(2\pi \hat{U}_2). \tag{5.12}$$

(iii) Repeating steps (i) and (ii) m-times, obtain $\hat{Z}_1, \ldots, \hat{Z}_m$. Using (5.7), compute $\hat{S}(t_1), \ldots, \hat{S}(t_m)$.

Note that having $k_l + 1$ in the numerator of (5.11) ensures that $\hat{U}_l > 0$. This is important, since in (5.12) we have $\ln(\hat{U}_1)$.

Here is an example of code which implements this recipe.

Listing 5.1   BSModel01.h

```
#ifndef BSModel01_h
#define BSModel01_h

using namespace std;
#include<vector>

typedef vector<double> SamplePath;                                    ❶

class BSModel                                                         ❷
{
   public:
      double S0, r, sigma;
      BSModel(double S0_, double r_, double sigma_)
         {S0 = S0_; r = r_; sigma = sigma_;
                              srand(time(NULL));}                     ❸
      void GenerateSamplePath(double T, int m, SamplePath& S);        ❹
};

#endif
```

Listing 5.2   BSModel01.cpp

```
#include "BSModel01.h"
#include <cmath>

const double pi=4.0*atan(1.0);                                        ❺
```

```
double Gauss()                                          ❻
{
    double U1 = (rand()+1.0)/(RAND_MAX+1.0);
    double U2 = (rand()+1.0)/(RAND_MAX+1.0);
    return sqrt(-2.0*log(U1)) * cos(2.0*pi*U2);
}

void BSModel::GenerateSamplePath
                (double T, int m, SamplePath& S)        ❹
{
    double St = S0;
    for(int k=0; k<m; k++)
    {
        S[k]= St*exp((r-sigma*sigma*0.5)*(T/m)
                        +sigma*sqrt(T/m)*Gauss());
        St=S[k];
    }
}
```

❶ A `SamplePath` is a vector of numbers of type `double`. By declaring `SamplePath` through `typedef`, from now on we can use `SamplePath` as any other standard type, for example, by declaring `SamplePath S;`

❷ The class stores the parameters $S(0), r, \sigma$. Here we declare all parameters as `public` in order to streamline the code and save space. These variables should be declared as `private` and introduced together with the corresponding `public` access functions. In this chapter we are going to cut many such corners in order to keep the code as short and transparent as possible.

❸ A computer can never generate a truly random number. The job of generating pseudo-random numbers is done by the `rand()` function. The command
`srand(time(NULL));`
sets the initial value, called a **seed**, for the iterative algorithm used by `rand()`. It is customary to use current time as the seed. We should not set the seed each time `rand()` is executed. This could spoil independence between samples. In our program we make sure that
`srand(time(NULL));`
is executed by placing it in the constructor of the class.

It is worthwhile to know that we can also choose a fixed seed. For example, for any constant integer `a`, if we write

```
srand(a);
```
then each time the program is executed it will generate the same sequence of pseudo-random numbers. This is often helpful when comparing results or debugging.

❹ `GenerateSamplePath()` generates a sample path using (5.7). Here
we intentionally pass `S` by reference in order not to create a new in-
stance of `S` each time the function is called. Since the function will be
executed many times, this will help to speed up our program.

❺ C++ does not have the constant π readily available. An easy way to get
around this is to compute $\pi = 4\arctan(1)$. Making `pi` a constant speeds
up computations, since it will not have to be computed each time we
call `Gauss()`.

❻ `Gauss()` generates $\hat{Z}$ using (5.12).

Now we write out the code for pricing path-dependent options using (5.9).
We show how to price an arithmetic Asian call with payoff function (5.3).

Listing 5.3   PathDepOption01.h

```cpp
#ifndef PathDepOption01_h
#define PathDepOption01_h

#include "BSModel01.h"

class PathDepOption
{
   public:
      double T;
      int m;
      double PriceByMC(BSModel Model, long N);        ❶
      virtual double Payoff(SamplePath& S)=0;         ❷
};

class ArthmAsianCall: public PathDepOption
{
   public:
      double K;
      ArthmAsianCall(double T_, double K_, int m_)
            {T=T_; K=K_; m=m_;}
      double Payoff(SamplePath& S);                   ❸
};

#endif
```

Listing 5.4 PathDepOption01.cpp

```cpp
#include "PathDepOption01.h"
#include <cmath>

double PathDepOption::PriceByMC(BSModel Model, long N)    ❶
{
   double H=0.0;
   SamplePath S(m);                                        ❹
   for(long i=0; i<N; i++)
   {
      Model.GenerateSamplePath(T,m,S);
      H = (i*H + Payoff(S))/(i+1.0);
   }
   return exp(-Model.r*T)*H;
}

double ArthmAsianCall::Payoff(SamplePath& S)               ❸
{
   double Ave=0.0;
   for (int k=0; k<m; k++) Ave=(k*Ave+S[k])/(k+1.0);
   if (Ave<K) return 0.0;
   return Ave-K;
}
```

❶ `PriceByMC()` is the main pricing function, which can be shared by different types of path-dependent options. It computes the price of an option using (5.9). We declare N as `long` since the number of sample paths needed for accurate computations could exceed the range of `int`.

❷ `Payoff()` is a virtual function. This means that `PriceByMC()` uses different payoffs, depending on the subclass of `PathDepOption`.

❸ The class `ArithmAsianCall` is used to price arithmetic Asian calls. The `Payoff()` function for this class is computed using (5.3).

❹ We initialise a single variable S or type `SamplePath`, which is then passed by reference to `GenerateSamplePath()` and `Payoff()`. This is important since passing by reference speeds up computations.

Listing 5.5 Main19.cpp

```cpp
#include <iostream>
#include "PathDepOption01.h"

using namespace std;
```

```
int main()
{
    double S0=100.0, r=0.03, sigma=0.2;
    BSModel Model(S0,r,sigma);                              ❶

    double T=1.0/12.0, K=100.0;
    int m=30;
    ArthmAsianCall Option(T,K,m);                           ❷

    long N=30000;
    cout << "Asian Call Price = "
        << Option.PriceByMC(Model,N) << endl;               ❸

    return 0;
}
```

❶ We initialise an object `Model` of class `BSModel`.

❷ We initialise an object `Option` of class `ArthmAsianCall`.

❸ Calling `Option.PriceByMC(Model,N)` executes the pricing function from the `PathDepOption` class.

We finish the section by observing that the code can be used to price European options, since setting $m = 1$ gives $t_1 = T$.

Exercise 5.1 Add a class to the code from Listings 5.2–5.5, to compute the prices of European call and put options.

5.3 Pricing error

The price estimator $\hat{H}_N(0)$ given in (5.9) depends on a sample, and hence contains an error. In this section we discuss how to estimate the size of such an error.

Let us use the notation

$$\hat{H}^i(T) = h(\hat{S}^i(t_1), \ldots, \hat{S}^i(t_m)), \qquad \text{for } i = 1, \ldots, N.$$

An unbiased estimator of the standard error of $\hat{H}_N(0)$ is

$$\hat{\sigma}_N = \sqrt{\frac{1}{N(N-1)} \sum_{i=1}^{N} (e^{-rT} \hat{H}^i(T) - \hat{H}_N(0))^2}.$$

After a couple of elementary transformations, we can rewrite $\hat{\sigma}_N$ in a form better suited for numerical applications

$$\hat{\sigma}_N = \frac{e^{-rT}}{\sqrt{N-1}} \sqrt{\frac{1}{N}\sum_{i=1}^{N}\hat{H}^i(T)^2 - \left(\frac{1}{N}\sum_{k=1}^{N}\hat{H}^i(T)\right)^2}. \qquad (5.13)$$

From (5.13), by the law of large numbers, we can see that for large N

$$e^{rT}\sqrt{N-1}\,\hat{\sigma}_N \approx \sqrt{\mathbb{E}(H(T)^2) - \mathbb{E}(H(T))^2} = \sqrt{\mathrm{Var}(H(T))},$$

hence

$$\hat{\sigma}_N \approx \frac{e^{-rT}}{\sqrt{N-1}}\sqrt{\mathrm{Var}(H(T))}. \qquad (5.14)$$

This means that $\hat{\sigma}_N$ converges to zero as we increase N, but this convergence is slow. For example

$$\hat{\sigma}_{100N} \approx \frac{1}{10}\hat{\sigma}_N,$$

which means that to reduce the error by one decimal point we need to make about 100 times more simulations.

Below we modify our code from Listings 5.3, 5.4 to compute $\hat{\sigma}_N$ using (5.13).

Listing 5.6   PathDepOption02.h

```
#ifndef PathDepOption02_h
#define PathDepOption02_h

#include "BSModel01.h"

class PathDepOption
{
    public:
        double T, Price, PricingError;
        int m;
        double PriceByMC(BSModel Model, long N);
        virtual double Payoff(SamplePath& S)=0;
};

class ArthmAsianCall: public PathDepOption
{
    public:
        double K;
        ArthmAsianCall(double T_, double K_, int m_)
```

❶

```
            {T=T_; K=K_; m=m_;}
        double Payoff(SamplePath& S);
};

#endif
```

Listing 5.7   **PathDepOption02.cpp**

```
#include "PathDepOption02.h"
#include <cmath>

double PathDepOption::PriceByMC(BSModel Model, long N)
{
    double H=0.0, Hsq=0.0;                                   ❷
    SamplePath S(m);
    for(long i=0; i<N; i++)
    {
        Model.GenerateSamplePath(T,m,S);
        H = (i*H + Payoff(S))/(i+1.0);
        Hsq = (i*Hsq + pow(Payoff(S),2.0))/(i+1.0);          ❸
    }
    Price = exp(-Model.r*T)*H;
    PricingError = exp(-Model.r*T)*sqrt(Hsq-H*H)/sqrt(N-1.0); ❹
    return Price;
}

double ArthmAsianCall::Payoff(SamplePath& S)
{
    double Ave=0.0;
    for (int k=0; k<m; k++) Ave=(k*Ave+S[k])/(k+1.0);
    if (Ave<K) return 0.0;
    return Ave-K;
}
```

❶ We add `Price` and `PricingError` as members of the class. After executing

  `Option.PriceByMC(Model,N);`

  the price and the pricing error will be stored inside of `Option`.

❷ `Hsq` will be used to compute $\frac{1}{N}\sum_{i=1}^{N}\hat{H}^{i}(T)^{2}$ from (5.13).

❸ We compute `H` and `Hsq` simultaneously. Using the same `S` for `H` and `Hsq` speeds up computations and improves accuracy.

❹ The pricing error is computed using (5.13).

There is no need to modify `BSModel01.h` or `BSModel01.cpp`.

We can add a new file, `Main20.cpp`, in which we modify the `main()` function from Listing 5.5 to include

```
cout << "Asian Call Price = "
<< Option.PriceByMC(Model,N) << endl
<< "Pricing Error = " << Option.PricingError << endl;
```

This computes the price and the pricing error.

5.4 Greek parameters

In this section we compute the Greek parameters using the Monte Carlo approach. We show how to compute the delta, leaving other parameters as exercises.

Let $u : \mathbb{R} \to \mathbb{R}$ be a function such that

$$H(0) = u(S(0)).$$

Assuming that $u(z)$ is differentiable, the Greek parameter **delta** is defined as

$$\delta = \frac{du}{dz}(S(0)).$$

To compute δ we use the fact that for sufficiently small ε

$$\frac{du}{dz}(S(0)) \approx \frac{u((1 + \varepsilon)S(0)) - u(S(0))}{\varepsilon S(0)}. \tag{5.15}$$

Since

$$u((1 + \varepsilon)S(0)) = e^{-rT} \mathbb{E}_Q \left(h((1 + \varepsilon)(S(t_1), \ldots, S(t_m))) \right)$$

$$\approx e^{-rT} \frac{1}{N} \sum_{i=1}^{N} h((1 + \varepsilon)(\hat{S}^i(t_1), \ldots, \hat{S}^i(t_m)))$$

$$=: \hat{H}_{\varepsilon,N}(0),$$

by (5.15), we can approximate δ using

$$\delta \approx \hat{\delta} = \frac{\hat{H}_{\varepsilon,N}(0) - \hat{H}_N(0)}{\varepsilon S(0)}, \tag{5.16}$$

We now write out the code for computing δ by means of Monte Carlo.

Listing 5.8 PathDepOption03.h

```
#ifndef PathDepOption03_h
#define PathDepOption03_h

#include "BSModel01.h"

class PathDepOption
{
   public:
      double T, Price, PricingError, delta;            ❶
      int m;
      virtual double Payoff(SamplePath& S)=0;
      double PriceByMC(BSModel Model, long N,
                            double epsilon);            ❷
};

class ArthmAsianCall: public PathDepOption
{
   public:
      double K;
      ArthmAsianCall
            (double T_, double K_, int m_)
            {T=T_; K=K_; m=m_;}
      double Payoff(SamplePath& S);
};

#endif
```

Listing 5.9 PathDepOption03.cpp

```
#include "PathDepOption03.h"
#include <cmath>

void Rescale(SamplePath& S, double x)                  ❸
{
   int m=S.size();
   for (int j=0; j<m; j++) S[j] = x*S[j];
}

double PathDepOption::PriceByMC(BSModel Model, long N,
                                   double epsilon)      ❷
{                                                       ❹
   double H=0.0, Hsq=0.0, Heps=0.0;
   SamplePath S(m);
   for(long i=0; i<N; i++)
```

```
    {
        Model.GenerateSamplePath(T,m,S);                            ❺
        H = (i*H + Payoff(S))/(i+1.0);
        Hsq = (i*Hsq + pow(Payoff(S),2.0))/(i+1.0);
        Rescale(S,1.0+epsilon);                                     ❻
        Heps = (i*Heps + Payoff(S))/(i+1.0);
    }
    Price = exp(-Model.r*T)*H;
    PricingError = exp(-Model.r*T)*sqrt(Hsq-H*H)/sqrt(N-1.0);
    delta = exp(-Model.r*T)*(Heps-H)/(Model.S0*epsilon);            ❼
    return Price;
}

double ArthmAsianCall::Payoff(SamplePath& S)
{
    double Ave=0.0;
    for (int k=0; k<m; k++) Ave=(k*Ave+S[k])/(k+1.0);
    if (Ave<K) return 0.0;
    return Ave-K;
}
```

❶ We add δ as a member of our class.

❷ We add ε as a variable of the function.

❸ `Rescale()` multiplies a sample path by a number.

❹ Heps is used to compute $\frac{1}{N} \sum_{i=1}^{N} h((1 + \varepsilon)(\hat{S}^i(t_1), \ldots, \hat{S}^i(t_m)))$.

❺ Note that we use the same sample path S for the computation of the price, pricing error and δ. This is important since it speeds up computations and improves accuracy.

❻ To compute Heps we use $(1 + \varepsilon)(\hat{S}^i(t_1), \ldots, \hat{S}^i(t_m))$, hence we rescale the sample path.

❼ δ is computed using (5.16).

By adding a new file, `Main21.cpp`, and inserting

```
double epsilon=0.001;
cout << "Asian Call Price = "
<< Option.PriceByMC(Model,N,epsilon) << endl
<< "Pricing Error = " << Option.PricingError << endl
<< "       delta = " << Option.delta << endl;
```

inside of its `main()` function, we compute and display the δ.

Exercise 5.2 Using the fact that

$$\frac{d^2u}{dz^2}(S(0)) \approx \frac{u\left((1+\varepsilon)S(0)\right) - 2u(S(0)) + u\left((1-\varepsilon)S(0)\right)}{(\varepsilon S(0))^2}$$

expand the code from Listings 5.8–5.9 to compute the Greek parameter **gamma**, $\gamma = \frac{d^2u}{dz^2}(S(0))$.

Exercise 5.3 Expand the code from Listings 5.8–5.9 to compute other Greek parameters, such as the vega, theta or rho.

5.5 Variance reduction

Let us start with an example. Suppose that we want to compute $\mathbb{E}(X)$ for some random variable X using Monte Carlo. Assume also that we have a random variable Y, which is 'close' to X, and that we know the expectation $\mathbb{E}(Y) = y$. Since

$$\mathbb{E}(X) = \mathbb{E}(X - Y) + y,$$

instead of computing $\mathbb{E}(X)$ directly, we can use Monte Carlo to compute $\mathbb{E}(X - Y)$. If Y is close to X, then the error of such computation should be small. We refer to Y as a **control variate** for X.

This method allows us to reduce the error of computation without increasing the number of simulations.

Exercise 5.4 Let Z be a random variable with normal distribution $N(0, \frac{1}{4})$. Let $X = \cos(Z)$ and $Y = 1 - \frac{1}{2}Z^2$. Using the fact that

$$\mathbb{E}(Y) = 1 - \frac{1}{2}\mathbb{E}(Z^2) = \frac{7}{8},$$

write a program which computes $\mathbb{E}(X)$, using Y as a control variate.

The idea behind the choice of Y as a control variate follows from the fact that by Taylor's expansion of $\cos(z)$, for small z,

$$\cos(z) \approx 1 - \frac{1}{2}z^2.$$

Let us explain how to find the price of a path-dependent option with a payoff function $h : \mathbb{R}^m \to \mathbb{R}$, using some other option as a control variate. Suppose that we have an option with a payoff function $g : \mathbb{R}^m \to \mathbb{R}$, which is close to h. We shall use

$$G(T) = g(S(t_1), \ldots, S(t_m)),$$

as the control variate for

$$H(T) = h(S(t_1), \ldots, S(t_m)).$$

We assume that we can compute $G(0)$ analytically, and express $H(0)$ as

$$H(0) = e^{-rT} \mathbb{E}_Q (H(T) - G(T)) + G(0). \qquad (5.17)$$

In the following version of the code the `PathDepOption` class from Listing 5.8 is modified to include a pricing function which uses (5.17).

Listing 5.10 PathDepOption04.h

```
#ifndef PathDepOption04_h
#define PathDepOption04_h

#include "BSModel01.h"

class PathDepOption
{
   public:
      double T, Price, PricingError;
      int m;
      virtual double Payoff(SamplePath& S)=0;
      double PriceByMC(BSModel Model, long N);
      double PriceByVarRedMC
              (BSModel Model, long N, PathDepOption& CVOption);
      virtual double PriceByBSFormula
              (BSModel Model){return 0.0;}
};

class DifferenceOfOptions: public PathDepOption
{
   public:
      PathDepOption* Ptr1;
      PathDepOption* Ptr2;
      DifferenceOfOptions(double T_, int m_,
                      PathDepOption* Ptr1_,
                      PathDepOption* Ptr2_)
         {T=T_; m=m_; Ptr1=Ptr1_; Ptr2=Ptr2_;}
      double Payoff(SamplePath& S)
```

❶ ❷ ❸ ❹ ❺

```
            {return Ptr1->Payoff(S)-Ptr2->Payoff(S);}                    ⑥
};

class ArthmAsianCall: public PathDepOption
{
   public:
      double K;
      ArthmAsianCall(double T_, double K_, int m_)
            {T=T_; K=K_; m=m_;}
      double Payoff(SamplePath& S);
};

#endif
```

Listing 5.11 **PathDepOption04.cpp**

```
#include "PathDepOption04.h"
#include <cmath>

double PathDepOption::PriceByMC(BSModel Model, long N)
{
   double H=0.0, Hsq=0.0;
   SamplePath S(m);
   for(long i=0; i<N; i++)
   {
      Model.GenerateSamplePath(T,m,S);
      H = (i*H + Payoff(S))/(i+1.0);
      Hsq = (i*Hsq + pow(Payoff(S),2.0))/(i+1.0);
   }
   Price = exp(-Model.r*T)*H;
   PricingError = exp(-Model.r*T)*sqrt(Hsq-H*H)/sqrt(N-1.0);
   return Price;
}

double PathDepOption::PriceByVarRedMC                                    ❶
      (BSModel Model, long N, PathDepOption& CVOption)
{
   DifferenceOfOptions VarRedOpt(T,m,this,&CVOption);                    ❼

   Price = VarRedOpt.PriceByMC(Model,N)
         + CVOption.PriceByBSFormula(Model);                            ❽

   PricingError = VarRedOpt.PricingError;                               ❾

   return Price;
}
```

```
double ArthmAsianCall::Payoff(SamplePath& S)
{
    double Ave=0.0;
    for (int k=0; k<m; k++) Ave=(k*Ave+S[k])/(k+1.0);
    if (Ave<K) return 0.0;
    return Ave-K;
}
```

❶ This is the pricing function in which we compute $H(0)$ using (5.17). CVOption plays the role of control variate.

❷ Options that can be used as control variates need to have an analytic pricing formula. Here we add a function in which we compute $G(0)$ from the Black–Scholes formula. We make this function virtual, since the formula may vary depending on the type of option.

❸ Not all path-dependent options can be priced analytically. Here we return 0.0 to allow for having a subclass of PathDepOption without a PriceByBSFormula() function.

❹ We add a class which combines two options with payoffs $H(T)$ and $G(T)$, and creates an option with payoff $H(T) - G(T)$.

❺ Pointers Ptr1 and Ptr2 refer to options with payoffs $H(T)$ and $G(T)$, respectively.

❻ The payoff is equal to $H(T) - G(T)$.

❼ We initialise an object VarRedOpt of class DifferenceOfOptions.
    The keyword **this** requires careful explanation. When an object of some class is used, then this appearing anywhere inside that class designates a pointer to that object. Here the pointer this appears inside the PathDepOption class (or more precisely, inside a function belonging to that class). Later on, inside the main() function in Listing 5.14, we will have an object Option declared by
ArthmAsianCall Option(T,K,m);
Because ArthmAsianCall is a subclass of the PathDepOption class, Option can be regarded as an object of the parent class. When
Option.PriceByVarRedMC(Model,N,CVOption);
is executed, the this pointer inside PriceByVarRedMC() will therefore be pointing to the Option object. When it is passed to the constructor function of the VarRedOpt class in
DifferenceOfOptions VarRedOpt(T,m,this,&CVOption);

the `Payoff()` function in the `VarRedOpt` class will produce the difference between the payoffs of `Option` and `CVOption`.

⑧ We compute $H(0)$ using (5.17). By calling `VarRedOpt.PriceByMC()`, $e^{-rT}E_*(H(T) - G(T))$ is computed using Monte Carlo. Then $G(0)$ is computed in `CVOption.PriceByBSFormula()` from an analytic formula.

⑨ Since $G(0)$ is computed analytically, the only source of error follows from the Monte Carlo computation of $e^{-rT}E_*(H(T) - G(T))$.

To apply this code we still need to choose a control variate and implement its `PriceByBSFormula()` function.

As an example for the variance reduction technique, we are going to price an arithmetic Asian call option with payoff function (5.3). As the control variate we choose a **geometric Asian call** option with payoff function

$$g(z_1, \ldots, z_m) = h^{\text{geom Asian call}}(z_1, \ldots, z_m) = \left(\sqrt[m]{\prod_{k=1}^{m} z_k} - K\right)^+. \quad (5.18)$$

Since the geometric average is often close to the arithmetic average, this choice seems a good idea, provided that we know how to compute $G(0)$ analytically.

It turns out that

$$G(T) = h^{\text{geom Asian call}}(S(t_1), \ldots, S(t_m))$$

can be written as

$$G(T) = \left(ae^{\left(r - \frac{b^2}{2}\right)T + b\sqrt{T}Z} - K\right)^+, \quad (5.19)$$

where Z has the standard normal distribution $N(0, 1)$, and $a, b \in \mathbb{R}$ are constants:

$$a = e^{-rT}S(0)\exp\left(\frac{(m+1)T}{2m}\left(r + \frac{\sigma^2}{2}\left(\frac{(2m+1)}{3m} - 1\right)\right)\right), \quad (5.20)$$

$$b = \sigma\sqrt{\frac{(m+1)(2m+1)}{6m^2}}.$$

For details of the derivation, see [BSM]. From (5.19) we can see that $G(T)$ can be regarded as a European call option on an asset with time 0 price a and volatility b, which means that

$$G(0) = C(a, K, T, b, r). \quad (5.21)$$

The formula for $C(a, K, T, b, r)$ is given in (4.1), hence $G(0)$ can be computed analytically.

We are now ready to present the code for pricing the geometric Asian call (5.19) by means of the analytic formula (5.21). This option will play the role of control variate when pricing arithmetic Asian calls.

Listing 5.12   GmtrAsianCall.h

```
#ifndef GmtrAsianCall_h
#define GmtrAsianCall_h

#include "PathDepOption04.h"

class GmtrAsianCall: public PathDepOption
{
   public:
      double K;
      GmtrAsianCall(double T_, double K_, int m_)
           {T=T_; K=K_; m=m_;}
      double Payoff(SamplePath& S);
      double PriceByBSFormula(BSModel Model);            ❶
};

#endif
```

Listing 5.13   GmtrAsianCall.cpp

```
#include <cmath>
#include "GmtrAsianCall.h"
#include "EurCall.h"

double GmtrAsianCall::Payoff(SamplePath& S)              ❷
{
   double Prod=1.0;
   for (int i=0; i<m; i++)
   {
      Prod=Prod*S[i];
   }
   if (pow(Prod,1.0/m)<K) return 0.0;
   return pow(Prod,1.0/m)-K;
}

double GmtrAsianCall::PriceByBSFormula(BSModel Model)    ❶
{
   double a = exp(-Model.r*T)*Model.S0*exp(             ❸
```

```
            (m+1.0)*T/(2.0*m)*(Model.r
            +Model.sigma*Model.sigma
              *((2.0*m+1.0)/(3.0*m)-1.0)/2.0));
   double b = Model.sigma
              *sqrt((m+1.0)*(2.0*m+1.0)/(6.0*m*m));
   EurCall G(T, K);                                          ❹
   Price = G.PriceByBSFormula(a,b,Model.r);                  ❺
   return Price;
}
```

❶ The option is priced by means of the analytic formula from the Black–
Scholes model, hence the pricing takes place in `PriceByBSFormula()`.

❷ Here we have the payoff (5.18).

❸ We compute the constants *a* and *b* from (5.20).

❹ We also declare G of class `EurCall`, a European call option to be priced
by (5.21).

❺ Here *G*(0) is computed from (5.21). The function
`EurCall::PriceByBSFormula()`
is implemented in Listing 4.8.

We are ready to price the arithmetic Asian call, using the geometric Asian
call as control variate.

Listing 5.14   Main22.cpp

```
#include <iostream>
#include "PathDepOption04.h"
#include "GmtrAsianCall.h"

using namespace std;

int main()
{
   double S0=100.0, r=0.03, sigma=0.2;
   BSModel Model(S0,r,sigma);

   double T =1.0/12.0, K=100.0;
   int m=30;

   ArthmAsianCall Option(T,K,m);                             ❶
   GmtrAsianCall  CVOption(T,K,m);

   long N=30000;
```

```
Option.PriceByVarRedMC(Model,N,CVOption);                    ❷
cout << "Arithmetic call price = " << Option.Price << endl
    << "Error = " << Option.PricingError << endl;

Option.PriceByMC(Model,N);                                   ❸
cout << "Price by direct MC = " << Option.Price << endl
    << "MC Error = " << Option.PricingError << endl;

return 0;
}
```

❶ `Option` is the arithmetic Asian call which we are going to price, and `CVOption` is the control variate.

❷ We price `Option` using the variance reduction technique, with control variate `CVOption`.

❸ We also price `Option` using the standard Monte Carlo method and display the error for comparison. In this particular example, the standard error of `PriceByVarRedMC()` is about 100 times smaller than the standard error of `PriceByMC()`. Note that the error has been reduced without increasing `N`.

Control variates can be used to compute the Greeks. We demonstrate how this can be done by using δ as an example. Let $u_H(z)$ and $u_G(z)$ denote functions such that $H(0) = u_H(S(0))$ and $G(0) = u_G(S(0))$, and let

$$\delta_H = \frac{du_H}{dz}(S(0)), \qquad \delta_G = \frac{du_G}{dz}(S(0)), \qquad \delta_{H-G} = \frac{d(u_H - u_G)}{dz}(S(0)).$$

Suppose that we know how to compute δ_G analytically. Since

$$\delta_H = \delta_{H-G} + \delta_G, \tag{5.22}$$

we can compute δ_{H-G} using Monte Carlo and thus obtain δ_H.

Exercise 5.5   Expand the code from Listings 5.10–5.14 to compute the δ of an arithmetic Asian call using (5.22). Use the fact that the δ of the geometric Asian call is $N(d_+^{a,b})\frac{a}{S(0)}$, where

$$d_+^{a,b} = \frac{\ln\frac{a}{K} + \left(r + \frac{b^2}{2}\right)T}{b\sqrt{T}}.$$

Exercise 5.6 Price a barrier call option with payoff function

$$h^{\text{barrier call}}(z_1, \ldots, z_m) = \mathbf{1}_{\{\max_{k=1,\ldots,m} z_k \le L\}} (z_m - K)^+,$$

using a call option with payoff function

$$g(z_1, \ldots, z_m) = h^{\text{call}}(z_1, \ldots, z_m) = (z_m - K)^+$$

as a control variate. Compute δ using (5.22).

Exercise 5.7 Price an arithmetic Asian call with payoff

$$H(T) = \left(\frac{1}{T} \int_0^T S(t)\,dt - K \right)^+,$$

using

$$G(T) = \left(\exp\left(\frac{1}{T} \int_0^T \ln S(t)\,dt \right) - K \right)^+$$

as a control variate. The price of the control variate can be computed using the fact that

$$G(T) = \left(c_1 e^{\left(r - \frac{c_2^2}{2} \right)T + c_2 \sqrt{T} Z} - K \right)^+,$$

where Z has standard normal distribution $N(0,1)$ and $c_1, c_2 \in \mathbb{R}$ are constants:

$$c_1 = S(0) e^{-\frac{1}{2}\left(r + \frac{\sigma^2}{6} \right)T}, \qquad c_2 = \frac{\sigma}{\sqrt{3}}.$$

5.6 Path-dependent basket options

In the multi-dimensional Black–Scholes model we have d stocks, whose time t prices we denote as $S_1(t), \ldots, S_d(t)$. We write

$$\mathbf{S}(t) = \begin{pmatrix} S_1(t) \\ \vdots \\ S_d(t) \end{pmatrix},$$

for the vector of prices at time t. The prices have the following dynamics under the risk-neutral probability:

$$S_j(t) = S_j(0) \exp\left(\left(r - \frac{\sigma_j^2}{2}\right)t + \sum_{l=1}^{d} c_{jl} W_l(t)\right), \qquad (5.23)$$

where $W_1(t), \ldots, W_d(t)$ are independent Wiener processes under the risk-neutral probability Q, $\mathbf{C} = (c_{jl})_{j,l=1}^{d}$ is a $d \times d$ matrix, and $\sigma_1, \ldots, \sigma_d \in \mathbb{R}$ are defined as

$$\sigma_j = \sqrt{c_{j1}^2 + \cdots + c_{jd}^2} \quad \text{for } j = 1, \ldots, d. \qquad (5.24)$$

For more details on the d-dimensional Black–Scholes model, see [BSM].

We consider a path-dependent option with payoff at time T of the form

$$H(T) = h(\mathbf{S}(t_1), \ldots, \mathbf{S}(t_m)),$$

where $t_k = \frac{k}{m}$ for $k = 1, \ldots, m$, and where h is a payoff function

$$h : \underbrace{\mathbb{R}^d \times \cdots \times \mathbb{R}^d}_{m} \to \mathbb{R}.$$

An example of such an option is the **arithmetic Asian basket call**

$$H(T) = \left(\sum_{j=1}^{d} \left(\frac{1}{m} \sum_{k=1}^{m} S_j(t_k)\right) - K\right)^+. \qquad (5.25)$$

To simplify C++ code we introduce some notation. For two vectors $\mathbf{v}, \mathbf{w} \in \mathbb{R}^d$ we write

$$\mathbf{vw} = \begin{pmatrix} v_1 w_1 \\ \vdots \\ v_d w_d \end{pmatrix}, \qquad \exp(\mathbf{v}) = \begin{pmatrix} e^{v_1} \\ \vdots \\ e^{v_d} \end{pmatrix}. \qquad (5.26)$$

Let

$$\mathbf{Z} = \begin{pmatrix} Z_1 \\ \vdots \\ Z_d \end{pmatrix}$$

denote a d-dimensional random variable with standard normal distribution $N(0, \mathbf{I})$, where $\mathbf{I}$ is a d-dimensional identity matrix. (In other words, $Z_1, \ldots, Z_d$ are i.i.d. random variables with distribution $N(0, 1)$.) Let

$$\mathbf{Z}_1, \ldots, \mathbf{Z}_m$$

be a sequence of i.i.d. random variables with distribution $N(0, I)$, and let

$$\sigma = \begin{pmatrix} \sigma_1 \\ \vdots \\ \sigma_d \end{pmatrix}.$$

Using (5.23) and notation (5.26), for $k = 1, \ldots, m$, the price vector $S(t_k)$ can be expressed as

$$S(t_k) = S(t_{k-1}) \exp\left(\left(r - \frac{1}{2}\sigma\sigma\right)(t_k - t_{k-1}) + \sqrt{t_k - t_{k-1}}\, CZ_k\right).$$

Let $\hat{Z}_1, \ldots, \hat{Z}_m$ be a sequence of independent samples of $Z_1, \ldots, Z_m$, respectively. We define a sample path

$$\left(\hat{S}(t_1), \ldots, \hat{S}(t_m)\right),$$

taking

$$\hat{S}(t_1) = S(0) \exp\left(\left(r - \frac{1}{2}\sigma\sigma\right)t_1 + \sqrt{t_1}\, C\hat{Z}_1\right), \tag{5.27}$$

$$\hat{S}(t_k) = \hat{S}(t_{k-1}) \exp\left(\left(r - \frac{1}{2}\sigma\sigma\right)(t_k - t_{k-1}) + \sqrt{t_k - t_{k-1}}\, C\hat{Z}_k\right),$$

for $k = 2, \ldots, m$.

Let $(\hat{S}^i(t_1), \ldots, \hat{S}^i(t_m))$, for $i = 1, \ldots, N$, be a sequence of independent sample paths. As for the Black–Scholes model with a single underlying asset, the price $H(0)$ of the option can be approximated by

$$H(0) \approx \hat{H}_N(0) := e^{-rT} \frac{1}{N} \sum_{i=1}^{N} h(\hat{S}^i(t_1), \ldots, \hat{S}^i(t_m)). \tag{5.28}$$

Below we implement (5.28). We start by setting up functions which will be used to handle matrix and vector operations.

Listing 5.15   Matrix.h

```
#ifndef Matrix_h
#define Matrix_h

#include <vector>
using namespace std;

typedef vector<double> Vector;
typedef vector<Vector> Matrix;
```

```
Vector operator*(const Matrix& C,const Vector& V);          ❷
Vector operator*(const double& a,const Vector& V);          ❹
Vector operator+(const double& a,const Vector& V);
Vector operator+(const Vector& V,const Vector& W);
Vector operator*(const Vector& V,const Vector& W);          ❺
Vector exp(const Vector& V);
double operator^(const Vector& V,const Vector& W);          ❻

#endif
```

Listing 5.16   Matrix.cpp

```
#include "Matrix.h"
#include <cmath>

Vector operator*(const Matrix& C,const Vector& V)           ❸
{
    int d = C.size();
    Vector W(d);
    for (int j=0; j<d; j++)
    {
        W[j]=0.0;
        for (int l=0; l<d; l++) W[j]=W[j]+C[j][l]*V[l];
    }
    return W;
}

...                                                          ❼

double operator^(const Vector& V,const Vector& W)           ❻
{
    double sum = 0.0;
    int d = V.size();
    for (int j=0; j<d; j++) sum = sum + V[j]*W[j];
    return sum;
}
```

❶ We declare types `Vector` and `Matrix` for vectors and matrices of type `double`.

❷ We declare various operators on vectors and matrices.
`Vector operator*(const Matrix& C,const Vector& V);`
will allow us to multiply a matrix by a vector. Thanks to this operator, for two vectors `W`, `V` and a matrix `C` we will be able to compute
`W = C * V;`

in C++ code. We pass variables by reference to speed up computations. The keyword **const** is used to ensure that the operators do not make any alterations to the variables passed to them.

❸ The result of multiplying a vector v by a matrix c is a vector. The C++ syntax for defining operators is almost identical to that used for functions.

❹ Here we have three very natural operators, which will allow us to multiply a vector by a number, add a number to a vector, and add two vectors.

❺ These operators will compute (5.26).

❻ This will be the scalar product. We use ^ since other C++ operators are already taken.

❼ All operators declared in Matrix.h are elementary. We omit the details for some of them in order not to fill up space with trivial code. The code can be found on the accompanying web page:
www.cambridge.org/9781107003712.

We now present the code which uses (5.27) to generate

$$\left(\hat{\mathbf{S}}^i(t_1), \ldots, \hat{\mathbf{S}}^i(t_m)\right).$$

Thanks to the various operators that have been defined, the code is compact and strongly resembles Listings 5.1, 5.2.

Listing 5.17   BSModel02.h

```
#ifndef BSModel02_h
#define BSModel02_h

#include "Matrix.h"

typedef vector<Vector> SamplePath;                              ❶

class BSModel
{
   public:
      Vector S0, sigma;
      Matrix C;
      double r;
      BSModel(Vector S0_, double r_, Matrix C_);                ❷
      void GenerateSamplePath(double T, int m, SamplePath& S);
};

#endif
```

Listing 5.18 BSModel02.cpp

```cpp
#include "BSModel02.h"
#include <cmath>

const double pi=4.0*atan(1.0);

double Gauss()
{
    double U1 = (rand()+1.0)/(RAND_MAX+1.0);
    double U2 = (rand()+1.0)/(RAND_MAX+1.0);
    return sqrt(-2.0*log(U1)) * cos(2.0*pi*U2);
}

Vector Gauss(int d)
{
    Vector Z(d);
    for (int j=0; j<d; j++) Z[j] = Gauss();
    return Z;
}

BSModel::BSModel(Vector S0_, double r_, Matrix C_)
{
    S0 = S0_; r = r_; C = C_; srand(time(NULL));
    int d = S0.size();
    sigma.resize(d);
    for (int j=0; j<d; j++) sigma[j] = sqrt(C[j] ^ C[j]);
}

void BSModel::GenerateSamplePath(double T, int m, SamplePath& S)
{
    Vector St = S0;
    int d = S0.size();
    for(int k=0; k<m; k++)
    {
        S[k]= St*exp((T/m)*(r+(-0.5)*sigma*sigma)
                    +sqrt(T/m)*(C*Gauss(d)));
        St=S[k];
    }
}
```

③

④

⑤

⑥

❶ Since our model can have more than one asset, a sample path will consists of a sequence of vectors.

❷ The constructor for the BSModel class depends on $S(0)$, r and $\mathbf{C}$. Based on these, all other parameters of the model can be computed.

❸ This function generates a sample of a *d*-dimensional random variable with normal distribution $N(0, \mathbf{I})$.

❹ The number of assets can be recovered from the dimension of $\mathbf{S}(0)$.

❺ To compute σ_j we use (5.24).

❻ Here we use (5.27). We now clearly see the benefits of using the various operators. Thanks to them `GenerateSamplePath()` is just as short as the function used for the Black–Scholes model with a single underlying asset.

Below we present code for pricing an arithmetic Asian basket call option with payoff (5.25). To keep the code as simple as possible we focus on option pricing and leave error estimation and computation of Greek parameters as exercises.

Listing 5.19 PathDepOption05.h

```
#ifndef PathDepOption05_h
#define PathDepOption05_h

#include "BSModel02.h"                                        ❶

class PathDepOption
{
   public:
      double T;
      int m;
      double PriceByMC(BSModel Model, long N);
      virtual double Payoff(SamplePath& S)=0;
};

class ArthmAsianCall: public PathDepOption
{
   public:
      double K;
      ArthmAsianCall(double T_, double K_, int m_)
            {T=T_; K=K_; m=m_;}
      double Payoff(SamplePath& S);
};

#endif
```

Listing 5.20   PathDepOption05.cpp

```cpp
#include "PathDepOption05.h"
#include <cmath>

double PathDepOption::PriceByMC(BSModel Model, long N)     ❷
{
   double H=0.0;
   SamplePath S(m);
   for(long i=0; i<N; i++)
   {
      Model.GenerateSamplePath(T,m,S);
      H = (i*H + Payoff(S))/(i+1.0);
   }
   return exp(-Model.r*T)*H;
}

double ArthmAsianCall::Payoff(SamplePath& S)              ❸
{
   double Ave=0.0;
   int d=S[0].size();
   Vector one(d);                                         ❹
   for (int i=0; i<d; i++) one[i]=1.0;
   for (int k=0; k<m; k++)
   {
      Ave=(k*Ave+(one^S[k]))/(k+1.0);                     ❺
   }
   if (Ave<K) return 0.0;
   return Ave-K;
}
```

❶ The code form Listing 5.19 is almost identical to Listing 5.3. The only difference is that we include `BSModel02.h` instead of `BSModel01.h`.

❷ The `PriceByMC()` function is identical to the one from Listing 5.4.

❸ Here we have the payoff (5.25).

❹ one is a d-dimensional vector, all of whose coordinates are equal to 1.

❺ Here we compute the arithmetic average from (5.25), taking advantage of the one vector and the scalar product to simplify the code.

Now we write out the `main()` function for path-dependent basket options.

Listing 5.21   Main23.cpp

```
#include <iostream>
#include "PathDepOption05.h"

using namespace std;

int main()
{
    int d=3;
    Vector S0(d);
        S0[0]=40.0;
        S0[1]=60.0;
        S0[2]=100.0;
    double r=0.03;
    Matrix C(d,d);
        C[0][0] =  0.1;  C[0][1] = -0.1;  C[0][2] = 0.0;
        C[1][0] = -0.1;  C[1][1] =  0.2;  C[1][2] = 0.0;
        C[2][0] =  0.0;  C[2][1] =  0.0;  C[2][2] = 0.3;
    BSModel Model(S0,r,C);

    double T=1.0/12.0, K=200.0;
    int m=30;
    ArthmAsianCall Option(T,K,m);

    long N=30000;
    cout << "Arithmetic Basket Call Price = "
        << Option.PriceByMC(Model,N) << endl;

    return 0;
}
```

❶ To keep data input within `main()` short, we consider a basket option with just three underlying assets, $d = 3$.

❷ We initialise a $d \times d$ matrix `C`.

❸ The three-dimensional Black–Scholes model is stored in `Model`.

❹ We initialise an object `Option` for an arithmetic Asian basket call option, and execute the pricing function.

Error estimation for basket options can be done using (5.13). We can use identical code to that in Listing 5.7. Of course we need to change
```
#include "PathDepOption02.h"
```
to
```
#include "PathDepOption05.h"
```
and make some cosmetic changes to `PathDepOption05.h`.

Exercise 5.8 Expand the code from Listings 5.19–5.21 to compute the pricing error.

We finish the chapter by discussing how to compute the Greeks for a basket option. We demonstrate this by means of an example, showing how to compute the δs corresponding to the underlying assets. Let

$$u(\mathbf{S}(0)) = u(S_1(0), \ldots, S_d(0)),$$

denote the price of the option dependent on the underlying asset prices. If $u(z_1, \ldots, z_d)$ is differentiable, then the deltas are defined as

$$\delta_j = \frac{\partial u}{\partial z_j}(S_1(0), \ldots, S_d(0)) \quad \text{for } j = 1, \ldots, d.$$

We write

$$(1 + \varepsilon_j) = \begin{pmatrix} 1 \\ \vdots \\ 1 \\ 1 + \varepsilon \\ 1 \\ \vdots \\ 1 \end{pmatrix},$$

for a vector, where $1 + \varepsilon$ is the jth coordinate. We also introduce the notation

$$(1 + \varepsilon_j)\hat{\mathbf{S}}(t_k) = \begin{pmatrix} \hat{S}_1(t_k) \\ \vdots \\ \hat{S}_{j-1}(t_k) \\ (1 + \varepsilon)\hat{S}_j(t_k) \\ \hat{S}_{j+1}(t_k) \\ \vdots \\ \hat{S}_d(t_k) \end{pmatrix}, \tag{5.29}$$

for $k = 1, \ldots, m$, and

$$\hat{H}_{\varepsilon_j, N}(0) = e^{-rT} \frac{1}{N} \sum_{i=1}^{N} h\big((1 + \varepsilon_j)\hat{\mathbf{S}}^i(t_1), \ldots, (1 + \varepsilon_j)\hat{\mathbf{S}}^i(t_m)\big).$$

With above notation, for small ε

$$\delta_j \approx \frac{u((1 + \varepsilon_j)\mathbf{S}(0)) - u(\mathbf{S}(0))}{\varepsilon S_j(0)},$$

hence

$$\delta_j \approx \hat{\delta}_j = \frac{\hat{H}_{\varepsilon_j,N}(0) - \hat{H}_N(0)}{\varepsilon S_j(0)}. \qquad (5.30)$$

Exercise 5.9 Expand the code from Listings 5.19–5.21 to compute the deltas using (5.30). Be sure to use the same samples while computing $\hat{\delta}_1, \ldots, \hat{\delta}_d$.

Exercise 5.10 Write a class for pricing of a European basket call option with payoff

$$H(T) = \left(\sum_{j=1}^{d} S_j(T) - K \right)^+.$$

Exercise 5.11 Use

$$G(T) = \sum_{j=1}^{d} \left(S_j(T) - K_j \right)^+, \qquad K_j = \frac{K S_j(0)}{\sum_{l=1}^{d} S_l(0)},$$

as a control variate to reduce the pricing error for the European basket call from Exercise 5.10.

6

Finite difference methods

6.1   Parabolic partial differential equations

Let us consider the parabolic partial differential equation

$$\frac{\partial v(t,x)}{\partial t} = a(t,x)\frac{\partial^2 v(t,x)}{\partial x^2} + b(t,x)\frac{\partial v(t,x)}{\partial x} + c(t,x)v(t,x) + d(t,x). \quad (6.1)$$

We look for a solution to (6.1) for $(t,x) \in [0,T] \times [x_l, x_u]$, with $x_l, x_u \in \mathbb{R}$ and $x_l < x_u$. To do so we need to impose the following boundary conditions:

$$v(T,x) = f(x), \quad (6.2)$$

$$v(t,x_l) = f_l(t), \quad (6.3)$$

$$v(t,x_u) = f_u(t), \quad (6.4)$$

where $f : [x_l, x_u] \to \mathbb{R}$ and $f_l, f_u : [0,T] \to \mathbb{R}$ are given functions. We refer to f as the **terminal boundary condition**, to f_l as the **lower boundary condition** and to f_u as the **upper boundary condition**.

A typical reason for studying (6.1) in finance is the Black–Scholes equation. Let $S(t)$ denote the price at time t of the underlying asset under the Black–Scholes model. Suppose that at time t the price of a financial derivative $H(t)$ can be expressed using a function $u : [0, T] \times \mathbb{R} \to \mathbb{R}$ as

$$H(t) = u(t, S(t)).$$

If u is a $C^{1,2}$ function on $[0, T) \times \mathbb{R}$, then

$$\frac{\partial u(t, z)}{\partial t} + \frac{\sigma^2}{2} z^2 \frac{\partial^2 u(t, z)}{\partial z^2} + rz \frac{\partial u(t, z)}{\partial z} - ru(t, z) = 0. \tag{6.5}$$

For more details see [BSM]. Equation (6.5) is a special case of (6.1), with coefficients

$$\begin{aligned}
a(t, z) &= -\frac{\sigma^2}{2} z^2, & b(t, z) &= -rz, \\
c(t, z) &= r, & d(t, z) &= 0.
\end{aligned} \tag{6.6}$$

We write $u(t, z)$ for a solution to the Black–Scholes equation (6.5) to distinguish it from $v(t, x)$ used for the general parabolic equation (6.1). We also write $h(z)$, $h_l(t)$, $h_u(t)$ for the boundary conditions for (6.5), to distinguish them from the boundary conditions $f(x)$, $f_l(t)$, $f_u(t)$ used for (6.1).

When $u(t, S(t))$ is the value of an option with expiry date T and payoff $H(T) = h(S(T))$, then $u(T, S(T)) = h(S(T))$, hence the terminal condition is

$$u(T, z) = h(z).$$

The lower and upper boundary conditions depend on the type of the option we wish to price. They can usually be derived from heuristic or arbitrage arguments.

For example, for a put option with expiry date T and strike price K, if $S(t)$ is high, then the option is practically worthless since it is unlikely to be exercised. This means that we can consider a sufficiently large z_u and set

$$u(t, z_u) = h_u^{\text{put}}(t) = 0. \tag{6.7}$$

If $S(t)$ is close to zero, then we can assume that we are almost certain to exercise the put at expiry and obtain a payoff close to K. Considering a sufficiently small positive z_l we can therefore set

$$u(t, z_l) = h_l^{\text{put}}(t) = e^{-r(T-t)} K. \tag{6.8}$$

Exercise 6.1 Using (6.7), (6.8) together with put–call parity, derive formulae for the upper and lower boundary conditions for a European call option.

Before discussing how to solve equation (6.1), we write out classes which will be used to store the coefficients and boundary conditions. As an example we consider the European put under the Black–Scholes model, leaving other options as exercises.

Listing 6.1   Option.h

```
#ifndef Option_h
#define Option_h

#include "BSModel01.h"                                            ❶

class Option                                                     ❷
{
   public:
      double T, zl, zu;                                          ❸
      virtual double Payoff(double z)=0;
      virtual double UpperBdCond
         (BSModel* PtrModel, double t)=0;                        ❹
      virtual double LowerBdCond
         (BSModel* PtrModel, double t)=0;
};

class Put: public Option
{
   public:
      double K;
      Put(double K_, double T_, double zl_, double zu_)
         {K=K_; T=T_; zl=zl_; zu=zu_;}
      double Payoff(double z);                                   ❺
      double UpperBdCond(BSModel* PtrModel, double t);
      double LowerBdCond(BSModel* PtrModel, double t);
};

#endif
```

Listing 6.2   Option.cpp

```
#include "Option.h"
#include <cmath>

double Put::Payoff(double z)                                     ❺
{
   if (K<z) return 0.0;
   return K-z;
}
```

```
double Put::UpperBdCond(BSModel* PtrModel, double t)        ❻
{
    return 0.0;
}

double Put::LowerBdCond(BSModel* PtrModel, double t)        ❼
{
    return K*exp(-PtrModel->r*(T-t));
}
```

❶ This is the file from Listing 5.1. Not all functionality in this class, for example `GenereateRandPath()`, is needed in the present chapter.

❷ The `Option` class includes virtual functions for the payoff and boundary conditions.

❸ We declare `T`, `zu`, and `zl` as `public` in order to streamline the code and save space. These variables should be declared as `private` and introduced together with the corresponding `public` access functions. In this chapter we are going to cut many such corners in order to keep the code as short and transparent as possible.

❹ A boundary condition often uses some parameters of the model. These will be passed using a pointer to an object of class `BSModel` containing these parameters.

❺ This is the payoff of the put $h^{\text{put}}(z) = (K - z)^+$.

❻ Here we have the upper boundary condition (6.7).

❼ The lower boundary condition is given by (6.8).

Now we introduce a general class for handling the coefficients of (6.1) and for the functions describing the boundary conditions, together with a subclass where we implement (6.5).

The class structure is depicted in Figure 6.1. In the diagram we find two relationships between classes. The one designated by an arrow represents the 'is a' relationship. For example, the Black–Scholes equation is a parabolic partial differential equation. The other one, depicted by a rhombus, represents the 'has a' relationship. The diagram indicates that `BSEq` has a pointer to `Option` and a pointer to `BSModel` among its members.

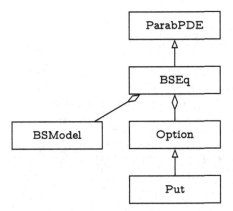

Figure 6.1 The `ParabPDE` and `BSEq` classes.

Listing 6.3 ParabPDE.h

```
#ifndef ParabPDE_h
#define ParabPDE_h

class ParabPDE                                          ❶
{
   public:
      double T,xl,xu;

      virtual double a(double t, double x)=0;
      virtual double b(double t, double x)=0;
      virtual double c(double t, double x)=0;
      virtual double d(double t, double x)=0;

      virtual double f(double x)=0;
      virtual double fu(double t)=0;
      virtual double fl(double t)=0;
};

#endif
```

Listing 6.4 BSEq.h

```
#ifndef BSEq_h
#define BSEq_h

#include "ParabPDE.h"
#include "BSModel01.h"
#include "Option.h"
```

```
class BSEq: public ParabPDE                                ❷
{
   public:
      BSModel* PtrModel;                                   ❸
      Option* PtrOption;                                   ❹
      BSEq(BSModel* PtrModel_,Option* PtrOption_);

      double a(double t, double z);
      double b(double t, double z);
      double c(double t, double z);
      double d(double t, double z);

      double f(double z);
      double fl(double t);
      double fu(double t);
};

#endif
```

Listing 6.5   BSEq.cpp

```
#include "BSEq.h"
#include <cmath>

BSEq::BSEq(BSModel* PtrModel_,Option* PtrOption_)          ❺
{
   PtrModel=PtrModel_; PtrOption=PtrOption_;
   T =PtrOption->T;
   xl=PtrOption->zl;
   xu=PtrOption->zu;
}

double BSEq::a(double t, double z)                         ❻
{
   return -0.5*pow(PtrModel->sigma*z,2.0);
}

double BSEq::b(double t, double z)                         ❻
{
   return -PtrModel->r*z;
}

double BSEq::c(double t, double z)                         ❻
{
   return PtrModel->r;
}
```

```
double BSEq::d(double t, double z)                    ❻
{
    return 0.0;
}

double BSEq::f(double z)                               ❼
{
    return PtrOption->Payoff(z);
}

double BSEq::fl(double t)                              ❼
{
    return PtrOption->LowerBdCond(PtrModel,t);
}

double BSEq::fu(double t)                              ❼
{
    return PtrOption->UpperBdCond(PtrModel,t);
}
```

❶ The `ParabPDE` class consists of virtual functions for the coefficients of (6.1) and for the functions describing the boundary conditions. It also contains T, xl, xu, which specify the domain $[0, T] \times [x_l, x_u]$.

❷ The class `BSEq` stores the coefficients and boundary conditions of the Black–Scholes equation (6.5).

❸ `PtrModel` will be used to pass the parameters of the model to the functions.

❹ The boundary conditions of `BSEq` will be computed based on the boundary conditions of the option pointed to by `PtrOption`.

❺ In the constructor we pass the pointers to the classes and initialise T, x_l, x_u.

❻ Here we have the coefficients (6.6) of the Black–Scholes equation.

❼ The boundary conditions are obtained from those of the option.

The code presented above does not yet allow us to solve (6.1). It serves only as a set-up for the methods introduced later on.

Exercise 6.2   Expand Listings 6.1 and 6.2 to include a European call option.

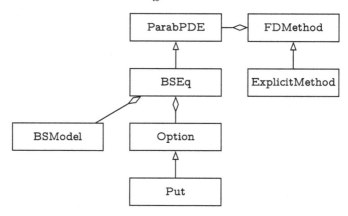

Figure 6.2 The `FDMethod` class communicates with the `BSEq` class through the `ParabPDE` class.

6.2 Explicit method

In the majority of cases finding an analytic solution to (6.1) with boundary conditions (6.2)–(6.4) is impossible. We shall present a method of finding a numerical solution of this problem on a finite set of points

$$\{(t_i, x_j) : i = 0, \ldots, i_{\max} \text{ and } j = 0, \ldots, j_{\max}\},$$

taking

$$
\begin{aligned}
t_i &= i\Delta t, & x_j &= x_l + j\Delta x, \\
\Delta t &= \frac{T}{i_{\max}}, & \Delta x &= \frac{x_u - x_l}{j_{\max}}.
\end{aligned}
\tag{6.9}
$$

For $i = 0, \ldots, i_{\max}$ and $j = 0, \ldots, j_{\max}$ we use the following notation:

$$v_{i,j} = v(t_i, x_j), \tag{6.10}$$

$$
\begin{aligned}
a_{i,j} &= a(t_i, x_j), & b_{i,j} &= b(t_i, x_j), \\
c_{i,j} &= c(t_i, x_j), & d_{i,j} &= d(t_i, x_j),
\end{aligned}
\tag{6.11}
$$

$$f_j = f(x_j), \qquad f_{l,i} = f_l(t_i), \qquad f_{u,i} = f_u(t_i). \tag{6.12}$$

Before presenting a numerical scheme for finding $v_{i,j}$, let us introduce a class which holds the functions (6.11), (6.12). The class structure is depicted in Figure 6.2, which is an extension of Figure 6.1.

Listing 6.6 FDMethod.h

```
#ifndef FDMethod_h
#define FDMethod_h
#include <vector>
#include "ParabPDE.h"                                            ①

using namespace std;
typedef vector<double> Vector;

class FDMethod
{
   public:
      ParabPDE* PtrPDE;                                          ②
      int imax, jmax;
      double dx, dt;

      vector<Vector> V;                                          ③

      FDMethod(ParabPDE* PtrPDE_, int imax_, int jmax_);

      double t(double i){return dt*i;}                           ④
      double x(int j){return PtrPDE->xl+dx*j;}

      double a(double i,int j){return PtrPDE->a(t(i),x(j));}     ⑤
      double b(double i,int j){return PtrPDE->b(t(i),x(j));}
      double c(double i,int j){return PtrPDE->c(t(i),x(j));}
      double d(double i,int j){return PtrPDE->d(t(i),x(j));}

      double f (int j){return PtrPDE->f(x(j));}                  ⑥
      double fu(int i){return PtrPDE->fu(t(i));}
      double fl(int i){return PtrPDE->fl(t(i));}

      double v(double t,double x);                               ⑦
};

#endif
```

Listing 6.7 FDMethod.cpp

```
#include "FDMethod.h"

FDMethod::FDMethod(ParabPDE* PtrPDE_, int imax_, int jmax_)
{
   PtrPDE=PtrPDE_;
   imax=imax_; jmax=jmax_;
```

```
    dx=(PtrPDE->xu - PtrPDE->xl)/jmax;                           ⑧
    dt=PtrPDE->T/imax;
    V.resize(imax+1);                                            ⑨
    for (int i=0; i<=imax; i++) V[i].resize(jmax+1);
}

double FDMethod::v(double t,double x)                            ⑦
{
    int i = (int)(t/dt);                                         ⑩
    int j = (int)((x-PtrPDE->xl)/dx);
    double l1 = (t-FDMethod::t(i))/dt, l0 = 1.0-l1;              ⑪
    double w1 = (x-FDMethod::x(j))/dx, w0 = 1.0-w1;
    return l1*w1*V[i+1][j+1] + l1*w0*V[i+1][j]                   ⑫
          +l0*w1*V[ i ][j+1] + l0*w0*V[ i ][j];
}
```

① The class `ParabPDE` from Listing 6.3 holds the coefficients $a(t, x)$, $b(t, x)$, $c(t, x)$ and $d(t, x)$ of (6.1). Based on these, the values $a_{i,j}, b_{i,j}, c_{i,j}$ and $d_{i,j}$ will be computed. `ParabPDE` also contains the boundary conditions, which will be used to compute f_j, $f_{l,i}$ and $f_{u,i}$.

② `PtrPDE` will be used to pass the functions from the `ParabPDE` class.

③ `V` is a matrix (declared as a vector of vectors) which will store the $v_{i,j}$ from (6.10).

④ `t(i)` and `x(j)` return t_i and x_j, respectively, using (6.9).

⑤ These functions return $a_{i,j}, b_{i,j}, c_{i,j}$ and $d_{i,j}$ using (6.11). Note that we declare `i` as `double`. This is done intentionally, since having fractional `i` will allow us to refine the method later on.

⑥ f_j, $f_{l,i}$ and $f_{u,i}$ are computed from (6.12).

⑦ Based on $v_{i,j}$, we can compute $v(t, x)$ for arbitrary $t \in [0, T]$ and $x \in [x_l, x_u]$ using linear interpolation. This will be the task of the function `v()`.

⑧ We compute Δx and Δt using (6.9).

⑨ `V` is resized to be an $(i_{max} + 1) \times (j_{max} + 1)$ matrix.

⑩ We choose i, j to represent a grid point approximating the given $t \in [t_i, t_{i+1}]$ and $x \in [x_j, x_{j+1}]$.

⑪ We find weights λ_0, λ_1 and ω_0, ω_1 such that $\lambda_0 + \lambda_1 = \omega_0 + \omega_1 = 1$ and (see Figure 6.3)

$$t = \lambda_0 t_i + \lambda_1 t_{i+1},$$
$$x = \omega_0 x_j + \omega_1 x_{j+1}.$$

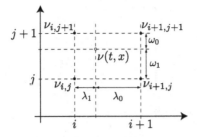

Figure 6.3 The value $v(t, x)$ can be approximated by a weighted average of $v_{i,j}, v_{i+1,j}, v_{i,j+1}$ and $v_{i+1,j+1}$.

We use $\texttt{FDMethod::t()}$ to avoid a clash between the function $\texttt{t()}$ and variable $\texttt{t}$. We treat $\texttt{x()}$ in the same fashion.

⑫ We approximate $v(t, x)$ by taking the weighted average (see Figure 6.3)

$$v(t, x) \approx \lambda_1 \omega_1 v_{i+1,j+1} + \lambda_1 \omega_0 v_{i+1,j} + \lambda_0 \omega_1 v_{i,j+1} + \lambda_0 \omega_0 v_{i,j}.$$

To compute $v(t_i, x_j)$ we need to discretise (6.1). For this we can use the approximations

$$\frac{\partial v(t_i, x_j)}{\partial t} \approx \frac{v_{i,j} - v_{i-1,j}}{\Delta t},$$

$$\frac{\partial v(t_i, x_j)}{\partial x} \approx \frac{v_{i,j+1} - v_{i,j-1}}{2\Delta x}, \qquad (6.13)$$

$$\frac{\partial^2 v(t_i, x_j)}{\partial x^2} \approx \frac{v_{i,j+1} - 2v_{i,j} + v_{i,j-1}}{\Delta x^2},$$

which follow from Taylor's expansion of $v(t, x)$ at (t_i, x_j); see Figure 6.4. Substituted into (6.1), these lead to the difference equation

$$\frac{v_{i,j} - v_{i-1,j}}{\Delta t} = a_{i,j} \frac{v_{i,j+1} - 2v_{i,j} + v_{i,j-1}}{\Delta x^2} + b_{i,j} \frac{v_{i,j+1} - v_{i,j-1}}{2\Delta x} + c_{i,j} v_{i,j} + d_{i,j}.$$

This equation can be reorganised as

$$v_{i-1,j} = A_{i,j} v_{i,j-1} + B_{i,j} v_{i,j} + C_{i,j} v_{i,j+1} + D_{i,j}, \qquad (6.14)$$

where

$$A_{i,j} = \frac{\Delta t}{\Delta x}\left(\frac{b_{i,j}}{2} - \frac{a_{i,j}}{\Delta x}\right), \qquad B_{i,j} = 1 - \Delta t\, c_{i,j} + \frac{2\Delta t\, a_{i,j}}{\Delta x^2},$$
$$C_{i,j} = -\frac{\Delta t}{\Delta x}\left(\frac{b_{i,j}}{2} + \frac{a_{i,j}}{\Delta x}\right), \qquad D_{i,j} = -\Delta t\, d_{i,j}. \qquad (6.15)$$

Some of the $v_{i,j}$ can be computed from the boundary conditions. By (6.2)

$$v_{i_{\max},j} = v(t_{i_{\max}}, x_j) = v(T, x_j) = f(x_j) = f_j, \qquad (6.16)$$

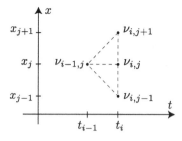

Figure 6.4 Explicit method follows from Taylor's expansion at (t_i, x_j).

for $j = 0, \ldots, j_{\max}$. By (6.3) and (6.4)

$$v_{i,0} = v(t_i, x_0) = v(t_i, x_l) = f_l(t_i) = f_{l,i}, \qquad (6.17)$$

$$v_{i,j_{\max}} = v(t_i, x_{j_{\max}}) = v(t_i, x_u) = f_u(t_i) = f_{u,i}, \qquad (6.18)$$

for $i = 0, \ldots, i_{\max} - 1$.

We can now find all $v_{i,j}$ using the following inductive steps, which need to be executed starting from $i = i_{\max}$ and finishing with $i = 0$:

(i) For $i = i_{\max}$, using (6.16) compute

$$v_{i_{\max},j} = f_j, \quad \text{for } j = 0, \ldots, j_{\max}. \qquad (6.19)$$

(ii) Using (6.17) and (6.18) compute $v_{i-1,0}$ and $v_{i-1,j_{\max}}$ as

$$v_{i-1,0} = f_{l,i-1}, \qquad (6.20)$$

$$v_{i-1,j_{\max}} = f_{u,i-1}. \qquad (6.21)$$

(iii) For $j = 1, \ldots, j_{\max} - 1$ compute $v_{i-1,j}$ using (6.14).

We can see that the above scheme allows us to compute $v_{i-1,j}$ explicitly, based on the values $v_{i,j}$ computed at time t_i (see Figure 6.4). It is known as the **explicit method**.

Below we write out the code in which we implement the method.

Listing 6.8 ExplicitMethod.h

```
#ifndef ExplicitMethod_h
#define ExplicitMethod_h

#include "FDMethod.h"
```

```
class ExplicitMethod: public FDMethod
{
   public:
      ExplicitMethod(ParabPDE* PtrPDE_, int imax_, int jmax_)
         : FDMethod(PtrPDE_, imax_, jmax_) {}            ❶

      double A(int i, int j)                              ❷
            {return dt*(b(i,j)/2.0-a(i,j)/dx)/dx;}
      double B(int i, int j)
            {return 1.0-dt*c(i,j)+2.0*dt*a(i,j)/(dx*dx);}
      double C(int i, int j)
            {return -dt*(b(i,j)/2.0+a(i,j)/dx)/dx;}
      double D(int i, int j)
            {return -dt*d(i,j);}

      void SolvePDE();                                    ❸
};

#endif
```

Listing 6.9 **ExplicitMethod.cpp**

```
#include "ExplicitMethod.h"

void ExplicitMethod::SolvePDE()                          ❸
{
   for (int j=0; j<=jmax; j++) V[imax][j]=f(j);          ❹
   for (int i=imax; i>0; i--)
   {
      V[i-1][0]=fl(i-1);                                 ❺
      V[i-1][jmax]=fu(i-1);
      for (int j=1;j<jmax;j++)
      {
         V[i-1][j]=A(i,j)*V[i][j-1]+B(i,j)*V[i][j]       ❻
                  +C(i,j)*V[i][j+1]+D(i,j);
      }
   }
}
```

❶ The constructor function of the `ExplicitMethod` class calls the constructor function of the parent class `FDMethod`. The syntax allows us to include additional code inside of `{}`. For our program this is not necessary.

❷ Here we have the coefficients $A_{i,j}$, $B_{i,j}$, $C_{i,j}$ and $D_{i,j}$ of the difference equation (6.14), computed using (6.15).

❸ This is the function in which we compute $v_{i,j}$ using (i)–(iii).

❹ We compute $v_{i_{\max},j}$ for $j = 0, \ldots, j_{\max}$ using (6.19).

❺ We compute $v_{i-1,0}$ and $v_{i-1,j_{\max}}$ using (6.20) and (6.21).

❻ We compute $v_{i-1,j}$ for $j = 1, \ldots, j_{\max} - 1$ using (6.14).

The program is almost complete. All that is left is to combine all components in the `main()` function.

Listing 6.10   Main24.cpp

```
#include <iostream>
#include "BSModel01.h"
#include "Option.h"
#include "BSEq.h"
#include "ExplicitMethod.h"

int main()
{
    double S0=100.0, r=0.05, sigma=0.2;
    BSModel Model(S0,r,sigma);                      ❶

    double K=100.0, T=1./12., zl=0.0, zu=2.0*S0;
    Put EuropeanPut(K,T,zl,zu);                     ❷

    BSEq BSPDE(&Model,&EuropeanPut);                ❸

    int imax=3000, jmax=1000;                       ❼
    ExplicitMethod Method(&BSPDE, imax, jmax);      ❹

    Method.SolvePDE();                              ❺

    cout << "Price = " << Method.v(0.0,S0) << endl; ❻

    return 0;
}
```

❶ `Model` is the Black–Scholes model with parameters $S(0)$, σ and r.

❷ `EuropeanPut` is the option that we wish to price.

❸ We initialise an object `BSPDE` of class `BSEq`. It contains functions which give the coefficients (6.6) of the Black–Scholes equation (6.5), together with the boundary conditions derived from `EuropeanPut` (see Listing 6.5).

❹ `Method` is the explicit method, with the aid of which we solve (6.5) with the corresponding boundary conditions, using (6.14). The coefficients (6.15) of (6.14) are computed using the functions from the `BSEq` class.

❺ Here we compute the $v_{i,j}$ using the explicit method. This is the main task of our program.

❻ We display the price $v(0, S(0))$.

❼ In order for our method to work we need to subdivide the time interval $[0, T]$ into a large number of parts. This is connected with the numerical stability of the method. For small i_{max}, errors can accumulate and blow up to produce invalid results. For the method to be stable, $\frac{\Delta t}{\Delta x^2}$ has to be sufficiently small.

Once we have computed the $v_{i,j}$, we can use (6.13) to approximate $\frac{\partial v(t_i,x_j)}{\partial x}$. This means that we can compute the replicating strategy using delta-hedging.

Exercise 6.3 Write functions based on $v_{i,j}$ to compute the replicating strategy.

Exercise 6.4 Modify the above program to price European call options using the explicit scheme. Compare with results obtained from analytic formulae. Experiment with different choices of i_{max} and j_{max} to see when the method becomes unstable.

We finish the section by showing that the explicit method can be expressed using matrix notation. Such notation will prove convenient in our later discussion.

Combining (6.14), (6.20) and (6.21) gives

$$\mathbf{v}_{i-1} = \mathbf{A}_i \mathbf{v}_i + \mathbf{w}_i, \tag{6.22}$$

where

$$\mathbf{v}_i = \begin{pmatrix} v_{i,1} \\ \vdots \\ v_{i,j_{\max}-1} \end{pmatrix}, \qquad \mathbf{w}_i = \begin{pmatrix} D_{i,1} + A_{i,1} f_{l,i} \\ D_{i,2} \\ \vdots \\ D_{i,j_{\max}-1} \\ D_{i,j_{\max}-1} + C_{i,j_{\max}-1} f_{u,i} \end{pmatrix}, \qquad (6.23)$$

$$\mathbf{A}_i = \begin{pmatrix} B_{i,1} & C_{i,1} & 0 & 0 & \cdots & & 0 \\ A_{i,2} & B_{i,2} & C_{i,2} & 0 & \cdots & & 0 \\ 0 & A_{i,3} & B_{i,3} & C_{i,3} & \ddots & & \vdots \\ 0 & 0 & \ddots & \ddots & \ddots & & 0 \\ \vdots & \vdots & \ddots & \ddots & \ddots & & C_{i,j_{\max}-2} \\ 0 & 0 & \cdots & 0 & A_{i,j_{\max}-1} & B_{i,j_{\max}-1} \end{pmatrix}. \qquad (6.24)$$

Note that the vectors $\mathbf{v}_i$ and $\mathbf{w}_i$ are of dimension $j_{\max} - 1$, and that the boundary conditions (6.20) and (6.21) are incorporated into the first and last coordinate of $\mathbf{w}_i$.

6.3 Implicit schemes

The main disadvantage of the explicit method is that it can become numerically unstable if the number of subdivisions of $[0, T]$ is too small. In this section we present an alternative approach, which leads to numerically stable methods.

The explicit method follows from the discretisation (6.13), which was used to transform (6.5) into the difference equation (6.14). Instead of (6.13) it is possible to use other discretisation schemes. We can choose

$$\begin{aligned} \frac{\partial v(t_{i-1}, x_j)}{\partial t} &\approx \frac{v_{i,j} - v_{i-1,j}}{\Delta t}, \\ \frac{\partial v(t_{i-1}, x_j)}{\partial x} &\approx \frac{v_{i-1,j+1} - v_{i-1,j-1}}{2\Delta x}, \\ \frac{\partial^2 v(t_{i-1}, x_j)}{\partial x^2} &\approx \frac{v_{i-1,j+1} - 2v_{i-1,j} + v_{i-1,j-1}}{\Delta x^2}, \end{aligned} \qquad (6.25)$$

which follows from Taylor's expansion of $v(t, x)$ at (t_{i-1}, x_j); see Figure 6.5.

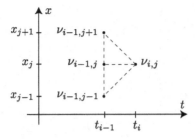

Figure 6.5 Implicit method follows from Taylor's expansion at (t_{i-1}, x_j).

Substituting (6.25) into (6.5) gives the difference equation

$$\frac{v_{i,j} - v_{i-1,j}}{\Delta t} = a_{i-1,j}\frac{v_{i-1,j+1} - 2v_{i-1,j} + v_{i-1,j-1}}{\Delta x^2} \tag{6.26}$$
$$+ b_{i-1,j}\frac{v_{i-1,j+1} - v_{i-1,j-1}}{2\Delta x} + c_{i-1,j}v_{i-1,j} + d_{i-1,j}.$$

In the equation we find $v_{i-1,j-1}$, $v_{i-1,j}$ and $v_{i-1,j+1}$, which means that we do not have an explicit formula for $v_{i-1,j}$ as was the case in (6.14). Because of this, (6.26) is referred to as the **implicit method**.

Depending on the choice of discretisation for $\frac{\partial v}{\partial t}$, $\frac{\partial v}{\partial x}$, $\frac{\partial^2 v}{\partial x^2}$, we can get other difference equations. We can, for example, choose the discretisation

$$\frac{\partial v\left(t_i - \frac{\Delta t}{2}, x_j\right)}{\partial t} \approx \frac{v_{i,j} - v_{i-1,j}}{\Delta t},$$
$$\frac{\partial v\left(t_i - \frac{\Delta t}{2}, x_j\right)}{\partial x} \approx \frac{1}{2}\left(\frac{v_{i,j+1} - v_{i,j-1}}{2\Delta x} + \frac{v_{i-1,j+1} - v_{i-1,j-1}}{2\Delta x}\right), \tag{6.27}$$
$$\frac{\partial^2 v\left(t_i - \frac{\Delta t}{2}, x_j\right)}{\partial x^2} \approx \frac{1}{2}\left(\frac{v_{i,j+1} - 2v_{i,j} + v_{i,j-1}}{\Delta x^2} + \frac{v_{i-1,j+1} - 2v_{i-1,j} + v_{i-1,j-1}}{\Delta x^2}\right),$$
$$v\left(t_i - \frac{\Delta t}{2}, x_j\right) \approx \frac{1}{2}\left(v_{i-1,j} + v_{i,j}\right),$$

which follows from Taylor's expansion of $v(t, x)$ at $(t_i - \frac{1}{2}\Delta t, x_j)$; see Figure 6.6.

Substituting (6.27) into (6.5) gives the difference equation

$$\frac{v_{i,j} - v_{i-1,j}}{\Delta t} = \frac{a_{i-1/2,j}}{2}\left(\frac{v_{i,j+1} - 2v_{i,j} + v_{i,j-1}}{\Delta x^2} + \frac{v_{i-1,j+1} - 2v_{i-1,j} + v_{i-1,j-1}}{\Delta x^2}\right)$$
$$+ \frac{b_{i-1/2,j}}{2}\left(\frac{v_{i,j+1} - v_{i,j-1}}{2\Delta x} + \frac{v_{i-1,j+1} - v_{i-1,j-1}}{2\Delta x}\right)$$
$$+ \frac{c_{i-1/2,j}}{2}\left(v_{i,j} + v_{i-1,j}\right) + d_{i-1/2,j}.$$

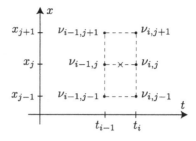

Figure 6.6 Crank–Nicolson method follows from Taylor's expansion at $(t_i - \frac{1}{2}\Delta t, x_j)$.

After reorganising, we obtain

$$E_{i,j}v_{i-1,j-1}+F_{i,j}v_{i-1,j}+G_{i,j}v_{i-1,j+1} = A_{i,j}v_{i,j-1}+B_{i,j}v_{i,j}+C_{i,j}v_{i,j+1}+D_{i,j}, \quad (6.28)$$

where

$$
\begin{aligned}
A_{i,j} &= \tfrac{\Delta t}{2\Delta x}\left(\tfrac{b_{i-1/2,j}}{2} - \tfrac{a_{i-1/2,j}}{\Delta x}\right), & E_{i,j} &= -A_{i,j}, \\
B_{i,j} &= \tfrac{\Delta t}{2}\left(\tfrac{2a_{i-1/2,j}}{\Delta x^2} - c_{i-1/2,j}\right) + 1, & F_{i,j} &= 2 - B_{i,j}, & (6.29) \\
C_{i,j} &= -\tfrac{\Delta t}{2\Delta x}\left(\tfrac{b_{i-1/2,j}}{2} + \tfrac{a_{i-1/2,j}}{\Delta x}\right), & G_{i,j} &= -C_{i,j}, \\
& D_{i,j} = -\Delta t\, d_{i-1/2,j}.
\end{aligned}
$$

This is known as the **Crank–Nicolson method**.

We shall explain how to compute $v_{i,j}$ using (6.28). The scheme will turn out to be indifferent to the choice of coefficients in (6.28). Since (6.26) can be reorganised in the form (6.28), with

$$
\begin{aligned}
A_{i,j} &= 0, & E_{i,j} &= -\tfrac{\Delta t}{\Delta x}\left(\tfrac{b_{i-1,j}}{2} - \tfrac{a_{i-1,j}}{\Delta x}\right), \\
B_{i,j} &= 1, & F_{i,j} &= 1 + \Delta t\, c_{i-1,j} - \tfrac{2\Delta t\, a_{i-1,j}}{\Delta x^2}, & (6.30) \\
C_{i,j} &= 0, & G_{i,j} &= \tfrac{\Delta t}{\Delta x}\left(\tfrac{b_{i-1,j}}{2} + \tfrac{a_{i-1,j}}{\Delta x}\right), \\
& D_{i,j} = -\Delta t\, d_{i-1,j},
\end{aligned}
$$

the scheme can also be applied for the implicit method.

In addition to (6.28), we have at our disposal the lower and upper boundary conditions

$$v_{i,0} = f_{l,i}, \quad (6.31)$$

$$v_{i,j_{\max}} = f_{u,i}. \quad (6.32)$$

Combining (6.28), (6.31) and (6.32), and using matrix notation, we obtain

$$\mathbf{B}_i \mathbf{v}_{i-1} = \mathbf{A}_i \mathbf{v}_i + \mathbf{w}_i, \tag{6.33}$$

where $\mathbf{A}_i$ is of the form (6.24) and

$$\mathbf{B}_i = \begin{pmatrix} F_{i,1} & G_{i,1} & 0 & 0 & \cdots & & 0 \\ E_{i,2} & F_{i,2} & G_{i,2} & 0 & \cdots & & 0 \\ 0 & E_{i,3} & F_{i,3} & G_{i,3} & \ddots & & \vdots \\ 0 & 0 & \ddots & \ddots & \ddots & & 0 \\ \vdots & \vdots & \ddots & \ddots & \ddots & & G_{i,j_{\max}-2} \\ 0 & 0 & \cdots & 0 & E_{i,j_{\max}-1} & & F_{i,j_{\max}-1} \end{pmatrix}, \tag{6.34}$$

$$\mathbf{v}_i = \begin{pmatrix} v_{i,1} \\ \vdots \\ v_{i,j_{\max}-1} \end{pmatrix}, \qquad \mathbf{w}_i = \begin{pmatrix} D_{i,1} + A_{i,1} f_{l,i} - E_{i,1} f_{l,i-1} \\ D_{i,2} \\ \vdots \\ D_{i,j_{\max}-2} \\ D_{i,j_{\max}-1} + C_{i,j_{\max}-1} f_{u,i} - G_{i,j_{\max}-1} f_{u,i-1} \end{pmatrix}. \tag{6.35}$$

We can now find all $v_{i,j}$ using the following inductive steps, which need to be executed starting from $i = i_{\max}$ and finishing with $i = 1$:

(i) For $i = i_{\max}$ compute $\mathbf{v}_{i_{\max}}$ from the terminal condition

$$v_{i_{\max},j} = f_j, \quad \text{for } j = 0, \ldots, j_{\max}. \tag{6.36}$$

(ii) Compute $\mathbf{v}_{i-1}$ from (6.33) as

$$\mathbf{v}_{i-1} = \mathbf{B}_i^{-1} \left(\mathbf{A}_i \mathbf{v}_i + \mathbf{w}_i \right). \tag{6.37}$$

(iii) Compute $v_{i-1,0}, v_{i-1,j_{\max}}$ using (6.31), (6.32).

We can see that in order to apply the method we need to be able to compute (6.37). To simplify the notation we consider a $d \times d$ matrix of the form

$$\mathbf{B} = \begin{pmatrix} F_1 & G_1 & 0 & \cdots & & 0 \\ E_2 & F_2 & G_2 & 0 & & \vdots \\ 0 & E_3 & F_3 & G_3 & & 0 \\ & & & & \ddots & \\ \vdots & \ddots & \ddots & \ddots & & G_{d-1} \\ 0 & \cdots & 0 & E_d & & F_d \end{pmatrix}, \tag{6.38}$$

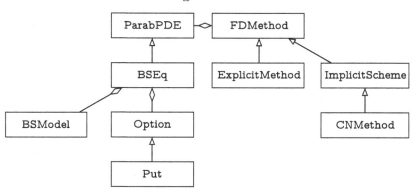

Figure 6.7 ImplicitScheme is a subclass of FDMethod.

and show how to compute

$$\mathbf{p} = \mathbf{B}^{-1}\mathbf{q} \tag{6.39}$$

for any vector $\mathbf{q} = (q_1, \ldots, q_d) \in \mathbb{R}^d$.

Lemma 6.1 LU decomposition
Let $\mathbf{B}$ be a matrix of the form (6.38) and let $\mathbf{q} \in \mathbb{R}^d$. If we take three vectors $\mathbf{p}, \mathbf{r}, \mathbf{y} \in \mathbb{R}^d$ defined as

$$r_1 = F_1, \qquad y_1 = q_1,$$
$$r_j = F_j - \frac{E_j}{r_{j-1}}G_{j-1}, \qquad y_j = q_j - \frac{E_j}{r_{j-1}}y_{j-1}, \qquad \text{for } j = 2, \ldots, d, \tag{6.40}$$

and

$$p_d = \frac{y_d}{r_d},$$
$$p_{j-1} = \frac{1}{r_{j-1}}\left(y_{j-1} - G_{j-1}p_j\right), \qquad \text{for } j = 2, \ldots, d, \tag{6.41}$$

then

$$\mathbf{p} = \mathbf{B}^{-1}\mathbf{q}.$$

The proof is given in Section 6.6.

Lemma 6.1 can be used to compute $\mathbf{B}^{-1}\mathbf{q}$ numerically. Starting with j equal to 1 and finishing with d, we first inductively compute r_j, y_j using (6.40). Then we inductively compute p_j using (6.41), starting with j equal to d and finishing with 1.

We are ready to write out the code in which we compute the $v_{i,j}$ using the steps (i)–(iii). The classes are depicted in Figure 6.7, which is an extension of Figure 6.2.

Listing 6.11 ImplicitScheme.h

```
#ifndef ImplicitScheme_h
#define ImplicitScheme_h

#include "FDMethod.h"
#include "Matrix.h"

class ImplicitScheme: public FDMethod
{
   public:
      ImplicitScheme(ParabPDE* PtrPDE_,int imax_,int jmax_)
         : FDMethod(PtrPDE_, imax_, jmax_){}

      virtual double A(int i, int j)=0;           ❶
      virtual double B(int i, int j)=0;
      virtual double C(int i, int j)=0;
      virtual double D(int i, int j)=0;
      virtual double E(int i, int j)=0;
      virtual double F(int i, int j)=0;
      virtual double G(int i, int j)=0;

      Vector w(int i);                            ❷
      Vector A(int i, Vector q);                  ❸

      Vector LUDecomposition(int i,Vector q);     ❹

      void SolvePDE();                            ❺
};
#endif
```

Listing 6.12 ImplicitScheme.cpp

```
#include "ImplicitScheme.h"
#include "Matrix.h"                              ❻
#include <cmath>

Vector ImplicitScheme::w(int i)                  ❷
{
   Vector w(jmax+1);                             ❼
   w[1]=D(i,1)+A(i,1)*fl(i)-E(i,1)*fl(i-1);
   for (int j=2;j<jmax-1;j++) w[j]=D(i,j);
   w[jmax-1]=D(i,jmax-1)+C(i,jmax-1)*fu(i)-G(i,jmax-1)*fu(i-1);
   return w;
}
```

```
Vector ImplicitScheme::A(int i, Vector q)                      ❸
{                                                               ❼
   Vector p(jmax+1);
   p[1]=B(i,1)*q[1]+C(i,1)*q[2];
   for (int j=2;j<jmax-1;j++)
   {
      p[j]=A(i,j)*q[j-1]+B(i,j)*q[j]+C(i,j)*q[j+1];
   }
   p[jmax-1]=A(i,jmax-1)*q[jmax-2]+B(i,jmax-1)*q[jmax-1];
   return p;
}

Vector ImplicitScheme::LUDecomposition(int i, Vector q)        ❹
{                                                              ❼
   Vector p(jmax+1), r(jmax+1), y(jmax+1);                     ❽
   r[1]=F(i,1);
   y[1]=q[1];
   for (int j=2;j<jmax;j++)
   {
      r[j]=F(i,j)-E(i,j)*G(i,j-1)/r[j-1];
      y[j]=q[j]-E(i,j)*y[j-1]/r[j-1];
   }
   p[jmax-1]=y[jmax-1]/r[jmax-1];                              ❾
   for (int j=jmax-2; j>0; j--)
   {
      p[j]=(y[j]-G(i,j)*p[j+1])/r[j];
   }
   return p;
}

void ImplicitScheme::SolvePDE()                                ❺
{
   for (int j=0; j<=jmax; j++) V[imax][j]=f(j);                ❿
   for (int i=imax; i>0; i--)
   {
      V[i-1]=LUDecomposition(i,A(i,V[i])+w(i));                ⓫
      V[i-1][0]=fl(i-1);                                       ⓬
      V[i-1][jmax]=fu(i-1);
   }
}
```

❶ These functions return $A_{i,j}, \ldots, G_{i,j}$. The scheme does not depend on the choice of the coefficients, hence we leave these functions as `virtual`.

❷ `w(i)` returns $\mathbf{w}_i$ from (6.35).

❸ `A(i,q)` returns $\mathbf{A}_i\mathbf{q}$ for $\mathbf{A}_i$ defined in (6.24).

❹ LUDecomposition(i,q) computes $\mathbf{B}_i^{-1}\mathbf{q}$ using Lemma 6.1.

❺ SolvePDE() is the function in which we compute the $v_{i,j}$ using (i)–(iii).

❻ This is the file from Listing 5.15. For our program we only need the operator + between two vectors. The operator is used in SolvePDE() for the computation of $\mathbf{A}_i\mathbf{v}_i + \mathbf{w}_i$.

❼ We declare the vectors to be of dimension $j_{max} + 1$, rather than $j_{max} - 1$ as is in (6.37). There are two reasons for doing so. Firstly, this way we have compatibility of dimension with V[i] in SolvePDE(). Secondly, this allows us to use the same indices in the code as in our formulae, which makes implementation more transparent. In all matrix operations needed for (6.37) we simply ignore the first coordinate $j = 0$ and the last coordinate $j = j_{max}$ of the vectors involved.

❽ The vectors $\mathbf{r}, \mathbf{y}$ are computed inductively using (6.40).

❾ The vector $\mathbf{p} = \mathbf{B}_i^{-1}\mathbf{q}$ is computed using (6.41).

❿ We apply (6.36) to compute $\mathbf{v}_{i_{max}}$.

⓫ We use (6.37) to compute $\mathbf{v}_{i-1}$.

⓬ We compute $v_{i,0}$ and $v_{i,j_{max}}$ using (6.31) and (6.32), respectively.

We now write out a class containing the coefficients (6.29) of the Crank–Nicolson method and then put the classes to work in the main() function.

Listing 6.13   CNMethod.h

```
#ifndef CNMethod_h
#define CNMethod_h

#include "ImplicitScheme.h"

class CNMethod: public ImplicitScheme
{
    public:
        CNMethod(ParabPDE* PtrPDE_,int imax_,int jmax_)         ❶
            : ImplicitScheme(PtrPDE_, imax_, jmax_) {}

        double A(int i, int j)                                  ❷
            {return 0.5*dt*(b(i-0.5,j)/2.0-a(i-0.5,j)/dx)/dx;}
        double B(int i, int j)
            {return 1.0+0.5*dt*(2.0*a(i-0.5,j)/(dx*dx)-c(i-0.5,j));}
        double C(int i, int j)
            {return -0.5*dt*(b(i-0.5,j)/2.0+a(i-0.5,j)/dx)/dx;}
        double D(int i, int j){return -dt*d(i-0.5,j);}
```

```
        double E(int i, int j){return -A(i,j);}
        double F(int i, int j){return 2.0-B(i,j);}
        double G(int i, int j){return -C(i,j);}
};

#endif
```

Listing 6.14   Main25.cpp

```
#include <iostream>
#include "BSModel01.h"
#include "Option.h"
#include "BSEq.h"
#include "CNMethod.h"

int main()
{
    double S0=100.0, r=0.05, sigma=0.2;
    BSModel Model(S0,r,sigma);

    double T=1./12., K=100.0, zl=0.0, zu=2.0*S0;
    Put EuropeanPut(K,T,zl,zu);

    int imax=200, jmax=2000;                              ❸

    BSEq BSPDE(&Model,&EuropeanPut);

    CNMethod Method(&BSPDE, imax, jmax);
    Method.SolvePDE();
    cout << "Price = " << Method.v(0.0,S0) << endl;

    return 0;
}
```

❶ We execute the constructor of `ImplicitScheme`.

❷ Here we have the coefficients from (6.29).

❸ For the Crank–Nicolson method we can choose much smaller `imax` than for the explicit method, without the method becoming unstable. This speeds up computations and allows for a choice of higher `jmax`, which improves accuracy.

Below we give two exercises for alternative implicit schemes. These can be implemented by adding classes analogous to `CNMethod` from Listing 6.13.

Exercise 6.5 Apply (6.30) to write a class for the implicit method (6.26).

Exercise 6.6 For any $\lambda \in (0,1)$, we can take a weighted average of (6.13) and (6.25), which leads to the approximation

$$\frac{\partial v(t_{i-\lambda}, x_j)}{\partial t} \approx \frac{v_{i,j} - v_{i-1,j}}{\Delta t},$$

$$\frac{\partial v(t_{i-\lambda}, x_j)}{\partial x} \approx \lambda \frac{v_{i-1,j+1} - v_{i-1,j-1}}{2\Delta x} + (1-\lambda)\frac{v_{i,j+1} - v_{i,j-1}}{2\Delta x},$$

$$\frac{\partial^2 v(t_{i-\lambda}, x_j)}{\partial x^2} \approx \lambda \frac{v_{i-1,j+1} - 2v_{i-1,j} + v_{i-1,j-1}}{\Delta x^2} + (1-\lambda)\frac{v_{i,j+1} - 2v_{i,j} + v_{i,j-1}}{\Delta x^2},$$

$$v(t_{i-\lambda}, x_j) \approx \lambda v_{i-1,j} + (1-\lambda) v_{i,j}.$$

Implement the method based on this approximation.

6.4 Changing coordinates

Partial differential equations are often solved through changes of coordinates. In this section we follow this approach for the Black–Scholes equation, which can be transformed into the much simpler heat equation.

We consider the change of coordinates

$$z = Z(t,x) = S(0)e^{\left(r-\frac{\sigma^2}{2}\right)t + \sigma x}, \tag{6.42}$$

$$v = V(t,u) = e^{-rt}u, \tag{6.43}$$

and define $v : [0,T] \times \mathbb{R} \to \mathbb{R}$ by

$$v(t,x) = V(t, u(t, Z(t,x))). \tag{6.44}$$

Proposition 6.2

If $u(t,z)$ is a solution to the Black–Scholes equation (6.5), then $v(t,x)$ defined in (6.44) satisfies

$$\frac{\partial v}{\partial t} = -\frac{1}{2}\frac{\partial^2 v}{\partial x^2}. \tag{6.45}$$

Moreover, the inverse change of coordinates to (6.42), (6.43) *is*

$$x = X(t, z) = \ln z - \left(r - \frac{\sigma^2}{2} \right) t, \qquad (6.46)$$

$$u = U(t, v) = e^{rt} v. \qquad (6.47)$$

The proof is given in Section 6.6.

We can see that (6.45) is much simpler than (6.5). Solving for $v(t, x)$ instead of $u(t, z)$ can improve the accuracy or stability of computations.

To solve (6.45) we need the corresponding boundary conditions. If $H(t) = u(t, S(t))$ is the price of an option with payoff $H(T) = h(S(T))$, then at maturity u is equal to $u(T, z) = h(z)$. This means that we should choose

$$f(x) = v(T, x) = V(T, u(t, Z(T, x))) = V(T, h(Z(T, x))) \qquad (6.48)$$

as the terminal boundary condition for (6.45).

By solving (6.45) on the domain $[0, T) \times [x_l, x_u]$, we obtain a solution of (6.5) on $\{(t, z) : t \in [0, T), z \in [Z(t, x_l), Z(t, x_u)]\}$. If x_l is sufficiently small and x_u is sufficiently large, then we can assume that

$$u(t, Z(t, x_l)) = h_l(t),$$
$$u(t, Z(t, x_u)) = h_u(t).$$

We therefore set the lower boundary condition as

$$f_l(t) = v(t, x_l) = V(t, u(t, Z(t, x_l))) = V(t, h_l(t)), \qquad (6.49)$$

and the upper boundary condition as

$$f_u(t) = v(t, x_u) = V(t, u(t, Z(t, x_u))) = V(t, h_u(t)). \qquad (6.50)$$

If we are interested in computing $u(0, z)$ for $z \in [z_l, z_u]$, then we can set

$$x_l = X(0, z_l), \qquad x_u = X(0, z_u). \qquad (6.51)$$

Since $z = 0$ is not in the domain of (6.46), we need to choose a positive z_l.

Once we have solved (6.45) to find $v(t, x)$, we can compute $u(t, z)$ using (6.46) and (6.47),

$$u(t, z) = U(t, v(t, X(t, z))). \qquad (6.52)$$

Now we give a class for (6.45), complete with the change of coordinates from (6.5) to (6.45). The class is included in Figure 6.8, which is an extension of Figure 6.7.

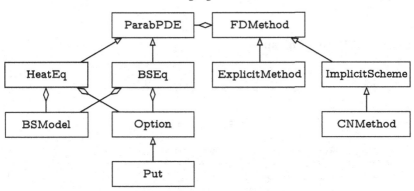

Figure 6.8 The HeatEq class is a subclass of the ParabPDE class.

Listing 6.15   HeatEq.h

```
#ifndef HeatEq_h
#define HeatEq_h

#include "BSModel01.h"
#include "Option.h"
#include "ParabPDE.h"

class HeatEq: public ParabPDE
{
   public:
      BSModel* PtrModel;
      Option* PtrOption;
      HeatEq(BSModel* PtrModel_,Option* PtrOption_);

      double a(double t,double x){return -0.5;}
      double b(double t,double x){return 0.0;}
      double c(double t,double x){return 0.0;}
      double d(double t,double x){return 0.0;}

      double f(double x);
      double fl(double t);
      double fu(double t);

      double Z(double t,double x);
      double V(double t,double u);
      double X(double t,double z);
      double U(double t,double v);
};

#endif
```

Listing 6.16 HeatEq.cpp

```cpp
#include "HeatEq.h"
#include <cmath>

HeatEq::HeatEq
(BSModel* PtrModel_,Option* PtrOption_)
{
   PtrModel=PtrModel_; PtrOption=PtrOption_;
   T=PtrOption->T;
   xl=X(0.0,PtrOption->zl);                                ❾
   xu=X(0.0,PtrOption->zu);
}

double HeatEq::f(double x)                                 ❷
{
   return V(T,PtrOption->Payoff(Z(T,x)));
}

double HeatEq::fl(double t)                                ❸
{
   return V(t,PtrOption->LowerBdCond(PtrModel,t));
}

double HeatEq::fu(double t)                                ❹
{
   return V(t,PtrOption->UpperBdCond(PtrModel,t));
}

double HeatEq::Z(double t,double x)                        ❺
{
   double r=PtrModel->r;
   double sigma=PtrModel->sigma;
   double S0=PtrModel->S0;
   return S0*exp((r-0.5*sigma*sigma)*t+sigma*x);
}

double HeatEq::V(double t,double u)                        ❻
{
   return exp(-PtrModel->r*t)*u;
}

double HeatEq::X(double t,double z)                        ❼
{
   double r=PtrModel->r;
   double sigma=PtrModel->sigma;
   double S0=PtrModel->S0;
   return (log(z/S0)-(r-0.5*sigma*sigma)*t)/sigma;
}
```

```
double HeatEq::U(double t,double v)                           ⑧
{
    return exp(PtrModel->r*t)*v;
}
```

❶ In (6.45) the coefficient $a(t, x)$ is equal to $-\frac{1}{2}$. The remaining coefficients are zero.

❷ This function computes the terminal boundary condition $f(x)$ for (6.45) using (6.48).

❸ This function computes the lower boundary condition $f_l(t)$ for (6.45) using (6.49).

❹ This function computes the upper boundary condition $f_u(t)$ for (6.45) using (6.50).

❺ $Z(t, x)$ is computed using (6.42).

❻ $V(t, u)$ is computed using (6.43).

❼ $X(t, z)$ is computed using (6.46).

❽ $U(t, v)$ is computed using (6.47).

❾ We specify the domain $[0, T] \times [x_l, x_u]$ for (6.45), choosing x_l and x_u according to (6.51).

Listing 6.17 Main26.cpp

```
#include <iostream>
#include "BSModel01.h"
#include "Option.h"
#include "HeatEq.h"
#include "CNMethod.h"

int main()
{
    double S0=100.0, r=0.05, sigma=0.2;
    BSModel Model(S0,r,sigma);

    double T=1./12., K=100.0, zl=1.0, zu=2.0*S0;    ❶
    Put EuropeanPut(K,T,zl,zu);

    int imax=200, jmax=2000;

    HeatEq HeatPDE(&Model,&EuropeanPut);            ❷
```

```
CNMethod Method(&HeatPDE, imax, jmax);
Method.SolvePDE();                                    ❸

double t=0.0;                                         ❹
double z=S0;

double x=HeatPDE.X(t,z);
cout << "Price = " << HeatPDE.U(t,Method.v(t,x)) << endl;  ❺

return 0;
}
```

❶ By choosing z_l small but greater than zero, we ensure that $\ln z$ in (6.46) is always well defined.

❷ In this class (6.45) is implemented together with the coordinate changes (6.42), (6.43), (6.46), (6.47).

❸ We solve (6.45) to find $v(t, x)$.

❹ We are going to compute $u(t, z)$ at $t = 0$ and $z = S(0)$.

❺ We use (6.52) to compute $u(t, z)$.

Exercise 6.7   Implement the change of coordinates

$$z = Z(x) = \frac{Lx}{1 - x},$$
$$v = V(z, u) = \frac{u}{z + L},$$

which transforms the Black–Scholes equation (6.5) into

$$\frac{\partial v}{\partial t} + \frac{\sigma^2}{2} x^2 (1 - x)^2 \frac{\partial^2 v}{\partial x^2} + rx (1 - x) \frac{\partial v}{\partial x} - (1 - x) rv = 0.$$

6.5 American options

Let $u(t, S(t))$ denote the price of an American option with a payoff function $h(z)$ and expiry date T, under the Black–Scholes model. Pricing the option can be formulated as a **linear complementarity problem** (LCP)[1]

$$\frac{\partial u(t,z)}{\partial t} + \frac{\sigma^2}{2}z^2\frac{\partial^2 u(t,z)}{\partial z^2} + rz\frac{\partial u(t,z)}{\partial z} - ru(t,z) \geq 0,$$

$$u(t,z) - h(z) \geq 0,$$

$$\left(\frac{\partial u(t,z)}{\partial t} + \frac{\sigma^2}{2}z^2\frac{\partial^2 u(t,z)}{\partial z^2} + rz\frac{\partial u(t,z)}{\partial z} - ru(t,z)\right)(u(t,z) - h(z)) = 0.$$

$$(6.53)$$

In general, the linear complementarity problem for the partial differential equation (6.1) can be written as

$$Lv(t,x) \geq 0, \qquad v(t,x) - g(t,x) \geq 0,$$
$$(Lv(t,x))(v(t,x) - g(t,x)) = 0,$$
$$(6.54)$$

where

$$Lv(t,x) = -\frac{\partial v(t,x)}{\partial t} + a(t,x)\frac{\partial^2 v(t,x)}{\partial x^2} + b(t,x)\frac{\partial v(t,x)}{\partial x} + c(t,x)v(t,x) + d(t,x).$$

We look for a solution to (6.54) on a finite domain $[0,T] \times [x_l, x_u]$, imposing the boundary conditions

$$v(T,x) = \max(f(x), g(T,x)),$$
$$v(t,x_l) = \max(f_l(t), g(t,x_l)),$$
$$v(t,x_u) = \max(f_u(t), g(t,x_u)).$$
$$(6.55)$$

If $v(t,x)$ satisfies (6.54), then we must either have $Lv(t,x) = 0$, meaning that the partial differential equation (6.1) is satisfied, or $v(t,x) = g(t,x)$. Thus, $g(t,x)$ implicitly defines a boundary condition for the equation $Lv(t,x) = 0$. We refer to $g(t,x)$ as the **free boundary condition**.

In this section we shall show how the problem (6.54) with boundary conditions (6.55) can be solved numerically, and apply the method to price American options.

With the aid of the discretisation (6.13), which was used for the explicit method, we can discretise $Lv(t,x)$ as

$$Lv(t_i, x_j) = v_{i-1,j} - \left(A_{i,j}v_{i,j-1} + B_{i,j}v_{i,j} + C_{i,j}v_{i,j+1} + D_{i,j}\right),$$

with $A_{i,j}, B_{i,j}, C_{i,j}, D_{i,j}$ given by (6.15). Problem (6.54) is then discretised

---

[1] For more details, see P. Wilmott, S. Howison and J. Dewynne, *The Mathematics of Financial Derivatives*, Cambridge University Press 1995.

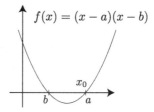

Figure 6.9 If $x_0 - a \geq 0$, $x_0 - b \geq 0$ and $(x_0 - a)(x_0 - b) = 0$, then $x_0 = \max\{a, b\}$.

as

$$v_{i-1,j} - \left(A_{i,j}v_{i,j-1} + B_{i,j}v_{i,j} + C_{i,j}v_{i,j+1} + D_{i,j}\right) \geq 0, \qquad v_{i-1,j} - g_{i-1,j} \geq 0,$$
$$\left(v_{i-1,j} - \left(A_{i,j}v_{i,j-1} + B_{i,j}v_{i,j} + C_{i,j}v_{i,j+1} + D_{i,j}\right)\right)\left(v_{i-1,j} - g_{i-1,j}\right) = 0, \quad (6.56)$$

where $g_{i,j} = g(t_i, x_j)$, with the corresponding boundary conditions

$$v_{i_{\max},j} = \max(f_j, g_{i_{\max},j}) \qquad \text{for } j = 0, \ldots, j_{\max},$$
$$v_{i-1,0} = \max(f_{l,i-1}, g_{i-1,0}), \qquad\qquad\qquad (6.57)$$
$$v_{i-1,j_{\max}} = \max(f_{u,i-1}, g_{i-1,j_{\max}}),$$

for $i = 1, \ldots, i_{\max}$.

This can be solved explicitly. We start with i equal to $i_{\max}$ and compute $v_{i_{\max},j}$ using (6.57), for $j = 0, \ldots, j_{\max}$. For a fixed i and for $j = 0, \ldots, j_{\max}$, once the $v_{i,j}$ are known, we can compute $v_{i-1,j}$ as (compare (6.56) with Figure 6.9)

$$v_{i-1,j} = \max\left\{\left(A_{i,j}v_{i,j-1} + B_{i,j}v_{i,j} + C_{i,j}v_{i,j+1} + D_{i,j}\right), g_{i-1,j}\right\}, \qquad (6.58)$$

for $j = 1, \ldots, j_{\max} - 1$, and compute $v_{i-1,0}$, $v_{i-1,j_{\max}}$ from (6.57). This allows us to compute $v_{i,j}$ inductively.

As an example, we apply the method to price an American put option under the Black–Scholes model.

We implement the method without making any changes to the existing files. The new classes are depicted in Figure 6.10. The idea is to make use of the ExplicitMethod class, where $A_{i,j}, B_{i,j}, C_{i,j}, D_{i,j}$ are already computed, by adding its subclass ExplicitLCP. Similarly, we add a subclass BSEqLCP of the BSEq class to access the coefficients of the Black–Scholes equation. The ExplicitLCP and BSEqLCP classes communicate through two additional classes named LCP and FDLCP. These are

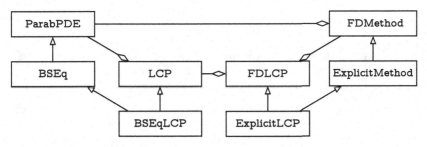

Figure 6.10 We shadow the existing code by adding subclasses and using pointers.

added to extend the functionality of the `ParabPDE` and `FDMethod` classes, respectively.

Listing 6.18   LCP.h

```
#ifndef LCP_h
#define LCP_h

#include "ParabPDE.h"

class LCP                                                    ❶
{
  public:
      ParabPDE* PtrPDE;
      virtual double g(double t,double x)=0;
};

#endif
```

Listing 6.19   BSEqLCP.h

```
#ifndef BSEqLCP_h
#define BSEqLCP_h

#include "LCP.h"
#include "BSModel01.h"
#include "Option.h"
#include "BSEq.h"

class BSEqLCP: public LCP, public BSEq             ❷
```

```
{
   public:
      BSEqLCP(BSModel* PtrModel,Option* PtrOption)               ❸
         : BSEq(PtrModel,PtrOption){PtrPDE = this;}

      double g(double t,double z)
         {return PtrOption->Payoff(z);}                          ❹
};

#endif
```

❶ The LCP class handles the coefficients of the LCP (6.54), together with the functions describing the boundary conditions. The majority of them, with the exception the free boundary condition, are passed to the class using a pointer to an object of ParabPDE class.

❷ The BSEqLCP class handles the LCP (6.53). Being a subclass of BSEq, it has access to the coefficients of the Black–Scholes equation.

❸ We execute the constructor of the BSEq parent class and set the pointer PtrPDE from the LCP parent class. Since BSEqLCP is a subclass of the ParabPDE class, the pointer this, which points to an object of class BSEqLCP, is also a pointer to an object of class ParabPDE.

❹ To price American options using the Black–Scholes equation we take $g(t,z) = h(z)$.

Listing 6.20   FDLCP.h

```
#ifndef FDLCP_h
#define FDLCP_h

#include "FDMethod.h"
#include "LCP.h"

class FDLCP                                                      ❶
{
   public:
      LCP* PtrLCP;                                               ❷
      FDMethod* PtrFDMethod;                                     ❸
      double g(int i,int j)                                      ❹
      {
         return PtrLCP->g(PtrFDMethod->t(i),PtrFDMethod->x(j));
      }
};

#endif
```

Listing 6.21 ExplicitLCP.h

```
#ifndef ExplicitLCP_h
#define ExplicitLCP_h

#include "LCP.h"
#include "FDLCP.h"
#include "ExplicitMethod.h"

class ExplicitLCP: public ExplicitMethod, public FDLCP       ❺
{
   public:
      ExplicitLCP(LCP* PtrLCP_, int imax_, int jmax_)
         : ExplicitMethod(PtrLCP_->PtrPDE, imax_, jmax_)       ❻
      {
         PtrLCP = PtrLCP_;                                     ❼
         PtrFDMethod = this;                                   ❽
      }

      void SolveLCP();                                         ❾
};

#endif
```

Listing 6.22 ExplicitLCP.cpp

```
#include "ExplicitLCP.h"

void ExplicitLCP::SolveLCP()                                  ❿
{
   for (int j=0; j<=jmax; j++)
   {
      V[imax][j]=f(j);
      if (V[imax][j]<g(imax,j)) V[imax][j]=g(imax,j);         ⓫
   }
   for (int i=imax; i>0; i--)
   {
      V[i-1][0]=fl(i-1);
      V[i-1][jmax]=fu(i-1);
      for (int j=1;j<jmax;j++)
      {
         V[i-1][j]=A(i,j)*V[i][j-1]+B(i,j)*V[i][j]
            +C(i,j)*V[i][j+1]+D(i,j);
      }
      for (int j=0;j<=jmax;j++)                                ⓬
      {
```

```
            if (V[i-1][j]<g(i-1,j)) V[i-1][j]=g(i-1,j);
        }
    }
}
```

❶ This class stores the coefficients of a discretised LCP.

❷ The pointer `PtrLCP` is used to gain access to the function $g(t, x)$ from the `LCP` class.

❸ We need the pointer `PtrFDMethod` to access the members of the `FDMethod` class.

❹ We compute $g_{i,j} = g(t_i, x_j)$ using the function `g()` from the `LCP` class, together with the functions `t()`, `x()` from the `FDMethod` class.

❺ The coefficients $A_{i,j}, B_{i,j}, C_{i,j}$ and $D_{i,j}$ of the discretised LCP (6.56) are computed from the same formulae as those of the explicit method. To gain access to them we make `ExplicitLCP` a subclass of the class `ExplicitMethod`. Making `ExplicitLCP` also a subclass of the `FDLCP` class gives access to the coefficient $g_{i,j}$.

❻ We execute the constructor of the `ExplicitMethod` class using the pointer `PtrLCP_->PtrPDE`.

❼ We set the pointer `PtrLCP` from the `FDLCP` parent class.

❽ To set the pointer `PtrFDMethod` from the `FDLCP` parent class we use the same technique which was used for the `LCP` and `BSEqLCP` classes.

❾ This function implements the method, and computes the $v_{i,j}$.

❿ The function `SolveLCP()` is very similar to `SolvePDE()` from Listing 6.9.

⓫ We compute $v_{i_{\max},j}$ from the terminal boundary condition (6.57).

⓬ This loop ensures that we apply (6.58) instead of (6.14), and that we compute the lower and upper boundary conditions using (6.57).

All that remains is to put the ingredients together inside the `main()` function.

Listing 6.23 Main27.cpp

```
#include <iostream>
#include "BSModel01.h"
#include "Option.h"
#include "BSEqLCP.h"
```

```
#include "ExplicitLCP.h"

int main()
{
    double S0=100.0, r=0.05, sigma=0.2;
    BSModel Model(S0,r,sigma);

    double K=100.0, T=1./12., zl=0.0, zu=2.0*S0;
    Put PutOption(K,T,zl,zu);

    BSEqLCP BSLCP(&Model,&PutOption);              ❶

    int imax=3000, jmax=1000;
    ExplicitLCP Method(&BSLCP, imax, jmax);        ❷

    Method.SolveLCP();                             ❸
    cout << "Am  Put Price = " << Method.v(0.0,S0) << endl;

    Method.SolvePDE();                             ❹
    cout << "Eur Put Price = " << Method.v(0.0,S0) << endl;

    return 0;
}
```

❶ We initiate an object BSLCP of class BSEqLCP.

❷ We initiate an object Method of class ExplicitLCP.

❸ We price the American put by solving the linear complementarity problem.

❹ Since ExplicitLCP is a subclass of the ExplicitMethod class, it can also be used to price European options.

Exercise 6.8 To price an American option with a payoff function $h(z)$ using the heat equation (6.45) we take

$$g(t, x) = V(t, h(Z(t, x))).$$

Implement a class, analogous to BSEqLCP, for handling coefficients of the linear complementarity problem for the heat equation. Use this class to price American and European put options.

The free boundary condition determines when an American option should be exercised. As long as

$$v(t, x) > g(t, x),$$

we should hold on to the option. If

$$v(t, x) = g(t, x),$$

then the option should be exercised.

Exercise 6.9   Write a function which given a point (t, x) determines if an American option should be exercised or not.

6.6   Proofs

Proof of Lemma 6.1   We need to show that

$$F_1 p_1 + G_1 p_2 = q_1, \tag{6.59}$$

$$E_j p_{j-1} + F_j p_j + G_j p_{j+1} = q_j \quad \text{for } j = 2, \dots, d-1, \tag{6.60}$$

$$E_d p_{d-1} + F_d p_d = q_d. \tag{6.61}$$

By (6.41) $p_1 = \frac{1}{r_1}(y_1 - G_1 p_2)$. Since r_1 and y_1 are chosen as $r_1 = F_1$ and $y_1 = q_1$, this gives (6.59).

Now we shall verify (6.60). By (6.40) we know that $\frac{E_j}{r_{j-1}} y_{j-1} = q_j - y_j$. Using (6.41), we therefore have

$$E_j p_{j-1} = \frac{E_j}{r_{j-1}}\left(y_{j-1} - G_{j-1} p_j\right) = q_j - y_j - \frac{E_j}{r_{j-1}} G_{j-1} p_j. \tag{6.62}$$

From (6.40)

$$F_j p_j = r_j p_j + \frac{E_j}{r_{j-1}} G_{j-1} p_j. \tag{6.63}$$

From (6.41) we have $p_j = \frac{1}{r_j}\left(y_j - G_j p_{j+1}\right)$, hence

$$G_j p_{j+1} = y_j - r_j p_j. \tag{6.64}$$

Adding (6.62), (6.63) and (6.64) gives (6.60).

Finally, let us check (6.61). Taking $j = d$, from (6.63) and the fact that $p_d = \frac{y_d}{r_d}$

$$F_d p_d = r_d p_d + \frac{E_d}{r_{d-1}} G_{d-1} p_d = y_d + \frac{E_d}{r_{d-1}} G_{d-1} p_d. \tag{6.65}$$

By (6.62), $E_d p_{d-1} = q_d - y_d - \frac{E_d}{r_{d-1}} G_{d-1} p_d$, which added to (6.65) gives (6.61).   □

Proof of Proposition 6.2   Equations (6.46) and (6.47) follow directly from (6.42) and (6.43).

By (6.47) and (6.44)

$$\frac{\partial u}{\partial z}(t,z) = \frac{d}{dz}U(t, v(t, X(t,z)))$$

$$= \frac{d}{dz}\left(e^{rt}v(t, X(t,z))\right) = e^{rt}\frac{\partial v}{\partial x}\frac{\partial X}{\partial z} = e^{rt}\frac{\partial v}{\partial x}\frac{1}{\sigma z}.$$

Similarly,

$$\frac{\partial^2 u}{\partial z^2} = \frac{d}{dz}\left(e^{rt}\frac{\partial v}{\partial x}\frac{1}{\sigma z}\right) = e^{rt}\frac{\partial^2 v}{\partial x^2}\frac{1}{(\sigma z)^2} - e^{rt}\frac{\partial v}{\partial x}\frac{1}{\sigma z^2},$$

and

$$\frac{\partial u}{\partial t}(t,z) = \frac{d}{dt}U(t, v(t, X(t,z)))$$

$$= \frac{d}{dt}\left(e^{rt}v(t, X(t,z))\right)$$

$$= re^{rt}v + e^{rt}\frac{\partial v}{\partial t} + e^{rt}\frac{\partial v}{\partial x}\frac{\partial X}{\partial t}$$

$$= re^{rt}v + e^{rt}\frac{\partial v}{\partial t} - e^{rt}\frac{1}{\sigma}\left(r - \frac{\sigma^2}{2}\right)\frac{\partial v}{\partial x}.$$

Inserting these into (6.5) and simplifying gives (6.45). $\square$

Index

Printed in the United States
By Bookmasters